The Psychology of Everyday Life

First published in 1921, *The Psychology of Everyday Life* covers the major portion of the field known as modern psychology. In this work the author has attempted to give such knowledge of modern psychology to enable the person in the street to take an intelligent interest in the psychological problems and discussions of the day. Today it can be read in its historical context.

The Psychology of Everyday Life

James Drever

Routledge
Taylor & Francis Group
LONDON AND NEW YORK

First published in 1921
by Methuen & Co. Ltd

This edition first published in 2025 by Routledge
4 Park Square, Milton Park, Abingdon, Oxon, OX14 4RN

and by Routledge
605 Third Avenue, New York, NY 10017

Routledge is an imprint of the Taylor & Francis Group, an informa business

Publisher's Note
The publisher has gone to great lengths to ensure the quality of this reprint but points
out that some imperfections in the original copies may be apparent.

Disclaimer
The publisher has made every effort to trace copyright holders and welcomes
correspondence from those they have been unable to contact.

A Library of Congress record exists under LCCN: 22000550

ISBN: 978-1-032-93156-2 (hbk)
ISBN: 978-1-003-56468-3 (ebk)
ISBN: 978-1-032-93167-8 (pbk)

Book DOI 10.4324/9781003564683

THE PSYCHOLOGY
OF EVERYDAY LIFE

JAMES DREVER
M.A., B.Sc., D.Phil., F.R.S.E.

DIRECTOR OF THE GEORGE COMBE PSYCHOLOGICAL LABORATORY,
THE UNIVERSITY OF EDINBURGH

FIFTH EDITION

METHUEN & CO. LTD.
36 ESSEX STREET W.C.
LONDON

First Published	.	.	.	.	.	May 5th	1921
Second Edition	.	.	.	.	.	October	1921
Third Edition	.	.	.	.	.	September	1922
Fourth Edition	.	.	.	.	.	January	1924
Fifth Edition	.	.	.	.	.		1927

PRINTED IN GREAT BRITAIN

PREFACE

THE Psychology of Everyday Life might rightly be considered as covering the major portion of the field of modern psychology. This fact the author has kept in view throughout. The time has now come when the ordinary educated man desires some closer acquaintance with this science, which has so long represented a rather mysterious region, into which he has hardly ever dared to seek to penetrate—an attitude encouraged by the apparent aloofness of the older psychology from the pursuits and interests of daily life. The aloofness has in recent times disappeared. The work of the modern psychologist touches daily life at many points. What one might designate the 'psychologist's creed' is no longer professed merely by the psychologist—the belief, that is, that for all those arts and sciences which are concerned with the human factor in the world process in any of its phases the science of psychology is as fundamental as is the science of physics for all those arts and sciences which are concerned with physical processes. The feeling of mystery too is fast yielding to a genuine desire for more knowledge.

This little book has been written with the object of satisfying this very reasonable desire. It is not an elementary textbook of psychology; nor is it a popular account of some of the marvels of psychology with all the psychology left out. It is popular, indeed, in the sense of being intended for the general reader, but from first to last it is a serious attempt to present, as far as possible in non-technical language, the main facts of the science so far as these touch the life of the man in the street. Difficulties are not slurred over or avoided, but faced, where the purpose of the work demanded that they should be faced. Technical and philosophical discussions alone are avoided, and the latter have really no place in psychology as a science in any case. To some extent the author has set before himself as a model Lewes's " Physiology of Common Life." How far he has fallen short of the qualities of that really excellent book, he is himself clearly conscious ; his aim, nevertheless, has been to do for the psychology of the present what Lewes did for the physiology of his time.

The topics which have been selected for treatment represent at one and the same time the essential elements of the science and those sections of it more particularly which have a close relation to practical life, and which in recent times have come prominently into notice in connexion with various developments in medicine, education, and industry. Possibly some readers may think that the latter have received less attention than they deserved. The Freudian reader more particularly will probably be of this opinion. The author has however striven to preserve a due balance of treatment in the science as a whole, and, taking the longer view, he is convinced that psychology is far wider than the theory of Freud or Jung, and that those psychologists themselves would be the first to acknowledge the fact. He has made a sincere attempt to place the various great advances of recent times in their due perspective in relation to a science which had already made notable advances before the able and enthusiastic workers of the present day were born. The absurd claim made on behalf of Freud's psychoanalysis by a recent writer, that it represents a new and distinct science, cannot for a moment be entertained. Freud's psychoanalysis is a method of psychological investigation—and of medical treatment—of very great value, it is granted, but its value must be assessed in the last resort by the science of psychology, not independently of that science. The appended bibliography will guide any reader who wishes to pursue the study of this or any other special topic beyond the limits fixed by the scope and intention of this little book, and in accordance with his own taste and inclination.

For the various facts, opinions, and lines of thought embodied in the work, the author would acknowledge his particular indebtedness to McDougall, Stout, Morton Prince, Titchener, William James, White, Pfister, and Freud. In most cases references are given to those works from which he has directly borrowed. For any omissions due to oversight he desires to express his regret.

J. D.

UNIVERSITY OF EDINBURGH
December, 1920

PREFATORY NOTE TO FOURTH EDITION

Some necessary notes have been added to the present edition. Otherwise there has been no change.

J. D.

EDINBURGH, *October, 1923.*

CONTENTS

CONTENTS

THE PSYCHOLOGY
OF EVERYDAY LIFE

CHAPTER I

INTRODUCTION

SOMETHING like a quarter of a century ago a leading American psychologist prophesied that, as the nineteenth century has been emphatically the century of physical science, so the twentieth century would be the century of psychology. The prophecy is in a fair way towards being fulfilled. At no time in the past has there been such a widespread interest in psychology, and at no time has more significant progress been made than during the last few years, in the direction of bringing psychology into touch with the needs and demands of practical life, and handing over to the psychologist for solution problems of the utmost importance for the welfare of humanity, which are quite obviously outside the sphere of any of the other sciences, physical or biological.

Though psychology is thus rapidly coming to its own at last, there is still unfortunately not a little confusion in the popular mind as to the exact nature and scope of the science, along with not a little doubt, and perhaps some mild curiosity, with regard to its votaries and their methods. The confusion, doubt, and curiosity are natural. Psychology is the daughter of philosophy, and has been so long and so carefully chaperoned by her mother that the notion of her appearing full-grown in an assembly of the sciences is a trifle disconcerting to those of the older generation who had a nodding acquaintance with the family, and mystifying to those, who, knowing the philosophy family only by sight or by repute, had always thought that there was little love lost between them and the sciences. Moreover, this adult and self-supporting daughter of philosophy has had the fortune—or the misfortune—to attract the admiring regards of a suitor, not too eligible, who has hitherto, indeed, shown little capacity for earning a living or for furnishing a home in the way a respectable science should, and has consequently been looked on askance and has incurred suspicion which has most undeservedly been passed on to her. The allusion is to psychical research in its spiritistic guise. The story is not a new one. The other sciences are also daughters of philosophy and elder sisters of psychology, though the fact is often forgotten to-day, and several of them had trouble with similarly ineligible suitors. They lived down unmerited suspicion and misunderstanding. So also will psychology.

Leaving figurative language aside, it is clear that any confusion and misconception regarding the nature and aim of psychology must first of all be removed, if this little book is to serve the purpose it is intended to serve. What then is psychology ? How would we define it as a science ? An answer to those questions ought to set matters right.

A science is best defined by specifying its subject-matter, the particular group of phenomena, or happenings, or processes in the universe, which it studies, and aims at reducing to some kind of scientific order. By the man in the street psychology would be defined as the science which studies the mind, and among psychologists of the older generation such a definition might have passed unchallenged. But science, if it has done nothing else, has at least made us critical of definitions. A moment's thought will show us that this is not a satisfactory description of the province of psychology. The province of a science should be described in terms of recognized distinctions and observed facts, in terms as free as possible from any implications or assumptions to which exception may be taken. To define psychology as the science of the mind implies that the mind is something which exists for itself, which may be very true, but is nevertheless a theoretical position many would deny. In any case the mind is not an observed fact ; it is something which, legitimately or not, we infer from observed facts.

There are really two possible ways of defining psychology, neither perhaps quite satisfactory or complete by itself, but yielding when combined a fairly adequate definition. We may define psychology as the science which studies mental or *psychical* facts or phenomena. Mental or psychical phenomena are such phenomena as desires, wishes, purposes, thoughts, beliefs, imaginings, recollections, perceptions, and the like—very real happenings taking place every day on a vast scale in this universe of ours. It is such phenomena, the conditions by which they are determined, the law and order which they manifest, that the psychologist certainly studies. But the objection suggests itself that these phenomena cannot be directly observed and studied except by each individual in his own experience, and a science claiming universal validity appears to be impossible on any such basis. Here the other method of defining the science comes to our aid. We may define psychology as the science which studies the behaviour of living organisms, and such a definition has met with considerable favour in recent years. Again there is no doubt that the psychologist does study the behaviour of living organisms. Nevertheless, this definition by itself is open to a serious objection from the opposite side, as it were. The facts of behaviour do constitute a group of facts which can be studied objectively and scientifically, but the science which studies behaviour will not be psychology except in so far as it regards behaviour as in some way the outcome of mental or psychical process. The truth is psychology studies the two groups of related facts, the facts of experience and the facts of behaviour. The objective happenings are those activities which constitute the behaviour of a living organism, but those objective happenings are interpreted in the light of that inside knowledge of the underlying mental processes or happenings, which each individual has direct access to in his own experience.

Such being the nature and scope of psychology, the question that next presents itself is: what is the use of psychology? What possible service can it render us to study psychology? The answer is not difficult. Our entire waking life is devoted to activities which realize certain aims, to the forming of resolutions or the carrying out of purposes. At least half—probably far more than half with most people—of our aims, resolutions, and purposes involve in a greater or less degree reference also to the activities of other people, involve co-operating with other people or opposing them, protecting them or protecting ourselves against them, advising or educating, checking or punishing them. Our whole active life, therefore, may be said to be devoted to the controlling and modifying of our behaviour by ourselves or others, or the controlling and modifying of the behaviour of other people by us, and we study behaviour in order through the better understanding of it to be able better to modify and control it.

It is not only on rare and important occasions, in the crises of our lives, that the need for understanding behaviour arises, but also in all the common actions of life, in what we do every day. When we try to induce a friend to do something with or for us, or to manage a servant, or to train a child, or to reclaim.one who has gone astray, we are trying to control or modify the behaviour of others ; when we strive to acquire some knowledge or a piece of skill, to learn to speak a foreign language or to play a sonata, to form or break a habit, we are striving to control or modify our own behaviour ; when we listen to a sermon at church, music at a concert, a play at the theatre, when we read a leading article, or see an advertising poster or hear a street vendor or newsboy, other people are trying to control or modify our behaviour. If we interpret behaviour so as to include all activity of the intellect or of the emotions, in addition to merely external behaviour, then, when we read a book, when we eat a dinner, when we hang a picture, we are exercising activities with which psychology is concerned, and about which psychology may be able to tell us a good deal. Thus in the ordinary affairs of everyday life we are continually meeting and solving psychological problems, and to some extent meeting and solving them in a psychological way. Most of us have some little inborn psychology. For is it not more or less a commonplace that nearly all success in dealing with other people depends on our being able to put ourselves in their places and see things with their eyes, which simply means interpreting their experiences from their behaviour, and forecasting their behaviour from our realization of their experiences ? And who among us is entirely incapable of this ?

But some one might turn round and say : " All this does not prove the use of psychology. Rather the reverse, if we have been doing these things all along without knowing psychology, except in this instinctive way. Besides, is it not the tactful person, rather than the psychologist, who is most successful in managing other people ? " Beginning with the last part of the objection, we should answer: " Undoubtedly, but the two are not mutually exclusive, for the tactful person may be also a psychologist, and, other things being equal, the psychologist is more likely to be tactful." The answer to the general objection may be made clear by an analogy. There is something wrong with our sewing machine. To all appearance it is something which, at least nine times before, we have put right in a certain way. We try that way now and only make things worse than ever, for this is the tenth case, and is quite different from the other nine, as a scientific knowledge of sewing machines would have told us—such a knowledge as is possessed by the expert who has to be called in to put matters right. Precisely similar is the case with the tactful person. In trying to ' manage ' some individual, he acts as he has done before in what seemed similar cases, and finds he is all wrong, and has only made things worse. Rule of thumb, or tact, or simple common sense may meet a situation nine times out of ten, and at the tenth fail because of lack of real scientific understanding of such situations, and unfortunately that tenth case may be the only critical case of the whole ten.   What seems, therefore, the strongest possible objection against the use value of psychology really leads to the strongest line of argument in its favour.

There is a third question which requires to be answered before the precise nature, scope, and place of psychology can be made clear.   There is obviously a group of real phenomena to be studied, and the value of scientific knowledge of these phenomena is granted, but by what methods of study can such a scientific knowledge be obtained ?   The methods employed by psychology are the methods employed by the other sciences—direct observation and experiment, in order to ascertain the facts, interpretation of and deduction from these facts in order to establish the laws.   Observation—experiment is nothing but observation under standard, controlled conditions—is directed towards mental processes themselves, and towards all mental expressions and products, including behaviour.   The direct observation of mental process is technically termed introspection—looking within. Obviously the only way to observe mental process directly is by looking within, and each individual, as we have already seen, can directly observe only his own mental processes. The observation of mental expressions and products is the normal kind of scientific observation, upon which other sciences also rely.

A great deal of unnecessary mystery has been made with regard to introspection, giving ordinary people the impression that to introspect is to do something very difficult on the one hand, and not without danger on the other, since, on the one hand, it requires a specially gifted mind, and on the other hand, tends to produce a morbid self-analysis. As a matter of fact we all introspect every day and every hour of our lives.   We can only interpret the behaviour of other people in terms of our own experience, and we can only use our own experience for this purpose by looking within.   In everyday life we are constantly inferring from the behaviour of other people their mental states, which according to our view explain that behaviour. Moreover, when we say of ourselves that we feel confused, or sad, or angry, that we are trying to recall something, or to make up our minds, we must have looked within in order to be able to make such a statement.

Introspection, therefore, is no great mystery, since it is something we are continually doing. Of course such introspection is not the systematic and trained introspection of the psychologist ; it is a very rough and ready introspection, often enough leading us to erroneous statements, as when we declare vehemently that we are not angry, while our whole appearance and behaviour show unmistakably that we are, or when we assert that we are trying to make up our minds, and, as the event shows, have had our minds made up all along, and are merely pretending to hesitate. It is true that the systematic use of introspection, as the psychologist uses it, requires practice and training, as is the case with the special method of any science. It is true also that its employment in some problems is very difficult ; analogies can again be found in other sciences. It is not true that there is anything occult about it. Any person of average intelligence can learn psychology, just as any such person can learn physics or chemistry. Of course some people will find introspection easier than others. But there is nothing unusual in that. Not every one possesses the natural bent and special capacity which make the expert physicist, or the expert chemist, any more than those which make the expert psychologist.

Introspection must be regarded as the final court of appeal in psychology, but, as we have seen, it is not the only method, nor is it the only source of psychological data. Observation of behaviour under experimental conditions, study of animal behaviour, study of the beliefs, customs, institutions, and life of various human societies and races at various stages of civilization and culture, require methods of observation other than introspection. The sources from which psychology obtains its data are exceedingly numerous. Everyday

I

life, fiction, history, child-study, physiology, zoology, anthropology are all laid under contribution, and all supply facts which the psychologist may and does utilize. The psychological interpretation of the facts must depend on introspection in the last resort, but to regard psychology as limited to facts which are open to introspection is an error of the first magnitude.

In order to clear the ground finally we may return to an earlier topic, and attempt to remove the confusion of psychology with philosophy on the one side and with spiritism on the other by showing briefly its relation to both. In describing psychology as a science with the attitude and method of science, we might be said to have done this already ; but a further brief statement of the exact position will not be out of place.

Take philosophy first. Time was, not so very long ago, when science put forward claims that involved the entire denial of philosophy. The scientists in effect maintained that all things in heaven and earth, God, immortality, the universe, and life, inspirations and ideals, everything high or humble, worthy or unworthy, noble or base, must submit to have its validity and even existence challenged, and established or the reverse, according to inexorable scientific laws. That time is past. Science now speaks in a different tone, acknowledging that scientific law is after all only hypothetical, that the scientific view of the universe is partial, abstract, and unreal. Science has become conscious that the scientific attitude means first of all assuming that we may treat the universe as a vast mechanism, and then proceeding to describe and explain that mechanism, which is obviously not the world of reality but a partial and abstract aspect of it, in which scientific law holds, mainly because it is itself the creation of science. Psychology as a science adopts precisely the same attitude. It says in effect that there is a certain group of phenomena which may be usefully and conveniently studied and explained on a scientific basis, and it proceeds to study them and explain them on this basis. Our consciousness of right and wrong, our ideals and our purposes, are from this point of view simply mental facts or phenomena. Psychology tries to give a scientific account of such things by abstracting this aspect, and regarding them purely as mental happenings of various kinds. To the chemist, so far as he is a chemist, lead is as interesting as gold. Similarly to the psychologist a bad act is on precisely the same footing as a good act, as regards its value. Both are phenomena of behaviour, and are studied as such without any reference to their moral quality, except so far as that is also a mental fact or phenomenon. In the same way for psychology beliefs are neither true nor false; they are simply mental facts to be explained by the operation of mental laws. In fine, psychology knows only cause and effect; it has nothing to do with ideals, values, purposes, and ends, except as mere facts of the mental life.

Philosophy is an attempt to get at the deeper reality of things. The significance of human life, the real nature of the soul, human destiny, immortality, God—these present problems for philosophy, not for psychology. It is probably true that the conclusions we arrive at in psychology may have an important bearing on our solution of some philosophical problems, but that is all we can say. An example will make the difference clear. Education is the most obvious case where psychology would seem to be directly applicable to the conduct of life. But there is a philosophy as well as a psychology of education. The primary and fundamental question to be settled in education is: what is to be our end or aim in educating? Psychology cannot attempt to answer such a question as that. It is a question involving ideals, aims, values, while psychology only deals with mental happenings as facts. It is a question in the answer to which the last word must lie with a philosophy of human life.

Turn now to spiritism. The situation is in some respects the same and in some respects different. To many of the claims of spiritism the psychologist would remain neutral, were he not directly challenged from the side of spiritism by other claims. That a human being goes on living after bodily death, and occasionally becomes manifest to those still in the flesh, may be a fact, but it is not a fact falling within the special domain of psychology. That a table is capable of such eccentric behaviour as hopping across a room on one leg, or a chair of flying up to the ceiling of its own accord, may be facts, but are not facts of a kind that concerns the psychologist. On the other hand, spiritists are very fond of invading the domain of psychology, and, as we shall see in a later chapter, of rioting in explanations of psychological phenomena which are not psychological. In such cases psychology cannot be neutral. If spiritism is right, psychology must be wrong.

To some extent, then, spiritist and psychologist may be dealing with the same phenomena. As examples of such phenomena we might cite hypnotism, changes of personality, automatic writing, dreams. What is the difference between the two attitudes in such cases ? Psychology, recognizing the duty of science to push its explanation of phenomena as far as the explanation will go, takes up the position that all such phenomena ought to be explained, and will ultimately be explained, on the same lines as other psychological phenomena. In any case such an attempt should be made, and the explanation must wait on the facts. Spiritism, on the other hand, comes to the facts with a ready-made explanation, citing them as evidence of powers and processes of which there is no trace in ordinary mental life. The psychologist, therefore, accepts in this field pretty much the same facts as the spiritist, but maintains that they can and will be psychologically explained—not of course that he can explain them—so as to show their complete continuity with the other phenomena of mental life.

CHAPTER II

THE FRAMEWORK OF EXPERIENCE

TO the series of mental happenings which any one individual can observe by looking within we give the name experience. Having now got some more or less adequate notion of the kind of science psychology is, we may enter on the definite psychological task of examining carefully the nature, and what we may call the framework, of experience. The tyro in psychology must be warned that this is by no means an easy quest. The present chapter is likely to prove the most difficult in the book. Yet the task must be undertaken, and ought not to be postponed. In psychology, if anywhere, what the first step costs is repaid a thousandfold in the confidence begotten of our success in taking that first step, and the deep, sure, and lasting insight into psychological problems to which it leads.

What experience is we all know directly and immediately. But we cannot define experience ; we cannot really describe it in any adequate way. Describing an experience and having the experience—living the experience—are worlds apart. Any description you or I or another may give of the colour blue or the pain of toothache falls utterly and hopelessly short of the reality of our experience of blue or the aching tooth. But, although we cannot adequately describe or define experience, the mere fact that we know our experience, as it were, from the inside enables us to make true statements about it, with the certain knowledge that they are true, and to avoid false notions about it by having the consciousness of their error forced upon us.

One erroneous idea about our experience which we are all very apt to have is to regard it as some kind of effect produced upon us by an external world acting through our sense organs, we ourselves being regarded as all the time passive recipients of the experiences. To say that this is the view of experience taken by the man in the street is to cast no slur on the intelligence of the man in the street. For in truth the view is a very tempting one, and philosophers and psychologists accepted it without demur for generations. It might, however, be as truly maintained that we make our own experience or that experience makes itself, by an activity, or through an activity, arising from within, as that we receive our experience passively from without. Neither statement represents the whole truth ; both err equally, though in contrary directions ; both emphasize one aspect and entirely neglect another aspect of experience. Experience is made partly from within and partly from without.

The best point of view from which to get a clear idea of the nature of experience, in the way in which the scientist regards it, is the point of view of the biologist, or rather the biological point of view. Man is a living organism. All living organisms, so long as they live, react to an environment. But the reaction is not the product entirely of the environment. The reaction is determined, on the one hand, by the life forces of the organism, on the other hand, by special features of the environment. Now experience is one way in which certain living organisms react to their environment. Hence it too should be determined partly by the life forces, partly by the environment.

Let us be perfectly clear on this point. It may seem unjustifiable to speak of experience as a reaction, since, as ordinarily understood, the reaction is really the external behaviour which experience prompts and guides. But a wider view shows that experience is itself a phase of the total reaction of the organism that terminates in the external behaviour. From the point of view of a hypothetical onlooker, who was capable of observing the whole fact of the reaction in all its phases, the experience would rightly be regarded as part of the reaction or response of the organism, though, from the point of view of the organism itself, and its fellow-organisms, only the behaviour should appear to be the reaction. The standpoint of science is that of the hypothetical observer of the whole fact. Hence for science experience is to be regarded as a phase in the reaction of the organism to its environment. Further, experience regarded as a phase in reaction to an environment, is a quite unique product of the life forces of the organism on the one side and the nature of the environment on the other. It is unique in that there is nothing else in the universe to which it can be compared. It is a compound product, or a synthetic product, to use chemical terminology, but a compound in which the life forces and the external environment take on the new character of mind. Such is experience from the biological point of view.

If we regard experience as a phase in the reaction of an organism to its environment, what may be described as its framework must consist of at least two distinct elements. There must be an element representing the life forces of the organism. This is sometimes plainly felt in the experience itself as a forward ' urge ' or ' drive,' and is present always, whether clearly discriminated or not, so long as there is reaction or response at all, that is, so long as there is life. The second element will represent the environment, or rather the effects produced on the organism by the nature of the environment. This will define the point at which, and the manner in which the reaction is to be made, and may be felt plainly in the experience as the hardness, or blueness, or shrillness, or ' pain-producingness ' of the environment, or something in the environment.

But there is in the framework of experience, or at least associated with the framework of experience, a third element which differs essentially from both these. It may be called even the central element or factor. Some psychologists would regard it as the peculiar characteristic which makes the whole phenomenon consciousness or mind. This is an excitement of the organism of the kind we usually call feeling, or sometimes emotion.   It plays the part of a regulating factor, functioning somewhat as the governor of a steam-engine.   The feeling may be agreeable or the reverse, very pronounced or scarcely discernible, but in any case it contributes to the experience its *meaning* for us personally and individually.

Hence the framework of experience consists of three constituent parts, the forward ' urge ' from within, the effect of the environment acting on the organism from without, the personal feeling giving the meaning of the whole.   The psychologist speaks of three ultimate modes of being conscious, knowing, feeling, and striving or willing.   To speak in such a way is somewhat misleading, for no experience is pure knowing, or pure feeling, or pure willing ; every experience is all three.   Knowing corresponds to the element representing conditions in the environment, feeling to the central and regulative factor, striving or willing to the inner force. In their most elementary and undeveloped forms the three elements may be said to be sensation, interest, and instinct. Here again instinct is the natural impulse to act coming from within, sensation the impression from without by which it is defined and guided, interest the excitement permeating the whole.   Every development of human knowledge, human character, and human conduct may be traced ultimately back to these three elements.

But how do these elements come to be bound together into anything we can rightly call a framework ?   The answer is to be found partly in the nature of experience or consciousness itself, and partly in the three general characters of all mental process which may be designated *conservation* or *retention, cohesion,* and *selection.*   As far as the nature of experience itself is concerned, we must take that for an ultimate datum.   An experience is actually and necessarily a synthetic product, as we have already pointed out.   But individual experiences make an experience, individual conscious processes make a consciousness, and that comes about through the three factors we have just mentioned, to which we must now direct attention.

Conservation or retention may be taken first. An experience is not something that simply happens and is done with, leaving the individual and the universe to which the individual belongs precisely as they were before. No event that takes place in the universe is like this. The whole universe has a history. But in the world of the inorganic or lifeless the after-results of an event may be so negligible, that the same event may occur over and over again without the bodies involved showing any material or perceptible alteration. The regularly recurring processes of nature are of this kind. The sun rises and sets and rises again, winter follows summer and summer follows winter once more, and for all practical purposes we may disregard any changes in earth and sun which have been brought about by any single one of these cycles. The case is different with a living organism. Everything that happens to it affects in a greater or less degree its whole subsequent history, for it has a history in a much more complete sense. Especially is this true where experience is involved. Every experience leaves behind some sort of ' trace ' which is conserved or retained, and which affects to a varying extent subsequent experience and subsequent behaviour. In fact we often use the word ' experience ' itself to denote this permanent something that is brought about by experiencing, and ' experience ' in this sense may itself be said to behave in a way almost exactly analogous to the behaviour of a living organism, as if it were, so to speak, an organism within an organism. Experience is itself living. At least it grows, and every stage in its growth develops out of the stage that preceded it. Whether it decays in the same way as a living organism decays is another matter. For practical purposes it may be said to exhibit decay, since we forget, or appear to forget, a great deal that we once knew. But, strictly speaking, such decay is due to the operation of quite different factors. In experience there is continuous development of every stage out of all the preceding stages from start to finish. So far as our present standpoint is concerned, there is one process, not two antagonistic processes.

But, leaving aside all analogy, we may say that it is characteristic of experience that some trace of it should be conserved permanently, so far as the lifetime of the organism is concerned. What is conserved is not the experience, but a definite change in the structure of the nervous system, and of the mind, brought about by the experience, what psychologists call a 'disposition.'[1]   It is this fact in the main that explains what we regard as the development of the mind, apart, that is to say, from the development involved in mere natural growth.   Through conservation or retention we rise unceasingly "on stepping stones of our dead selves."   It would be nearer the truth to say that the self of the past does not die, but lives on in the self of the present.   There is good—though not perhaps conclusive—evidence that no part of the experience of a self, not even the most insignificant, but affects the living self of the present, and is remembered by the self of the present, though it may be beyond specific recall.   However, we shall return to this topic later.

The second character of all mental process is what we have called cohesion.   The usual psychological term is *association*.   What we experience from moment to moment must not be regarded as a series of isolated items.   All the items cohere to a greater or less extent, so that there is, as it were, a thread—or rather many threads—of continuity running through all.   This is really involved in what has been said regarding conservation.   Illustrations which bring the fact of cohesion most forcibly home to us are to be obtained in any number from our everyday experience.   Consider what happens when we try to recall something, when we have mislaid a key, or a book, or a paper, let us say. We picture ourselves back at the moment when we last

---

[1] 'Disposition' is a technical term used by psychologists to denote a definite structural arrangement of mental and nervous elements in virtue of which we experience and act in a particular way.   Such 'dispositions' may be either inherited or acquired in the course of the individual life, or inherited 'dispositions' may be modified through experience.

had it, and proceed to trace in as great detail as possible
our doings since that time, or at least during the immediately
succeeding period. The wonderful unrolling of the past
that then occurs is so ordinary and frequent an event that
we have ceased to be sufficiently conscious of the wonder of
it to give even a moderate degree of attention to the mental
process, but reserve our whole attention for the end we have
in view. The unrolling can only take place because the
items of our experience have cohered in such a way that A
is linked to B, B to C, C to D, and so on, in the order in
which A, B, C and D originally occurred in our experience,
and now the thought of A immediately ushers into consciousness the thought of B, that the thought of C, that the thought
of D, carrying us right on perhaps to the thought of the
moment and of the event X, which terminates our quest
in the recovery of the key, book, or paper. Our whole
experience, retained as dispositions, is shot through and
through with these connexions due to cohesion, and every
train of ideas, every wandering thought even, may lay down
connexions in the most intricate way within the mass of
conserved material representing our past experience.

The third character of all mental process is selection. This
character depends to a greater extent than the other two
upon, and shows more clearly, the influence of the inward
'urge,' and the central regulative meaning, which we have
already discussed, though the way in which cohesion operates can also be shown to depend largely on these factors.
Not everything that happens to us plays the same part in
our experience, our memory, and our life. We are continually
selecting certain occurrences to be attended to and dwelt upon,
to form the main features of our inner history, while others
are passed lightly by. What guides and controls the selecting
will appear presently. In the meantime we are concerned
with the simple fact of selection, the fact that certain things
loom large in our experience at every moment of our existence,
it may be to sink into insignificance the next moment, as
some feature of our environment hitherto unnoticed springs
into prominence with a suddenness and overwhelmingness

that words utterly fail to express. In virtue of this selection experience is no monotonous series of items strung or cohering together, all of the same shape, colour, and liveliness, but some of the items are tingling and pulsating with the life itself, others are mere ordinary humdrum affairs, others hardly noticed at all. All degrees of selectiveness may be found, but in some degree or other experience is selective throughout. As mental development proceeds, selection comes to play a more and more important part in mental life. Upon it all the higher intellectual functions depend, while it is the alpha and omega of all moral development—in any strict sense of ' moral '—from its initial stages in the earliest beginnings of self-control in the child to its final stages in the aims and ideals of the completely civilized, socialized, and humanized adult.

CHAPTER III

APPETITES AND INSTINCTS

MAN is primarily a doer rather than a knower, and his knowing is for the sake of, and with reference to, what he is doing or means to do. The psychology of man as a pure intellect is a thing of the past. The psychology of the present studies human nature as it is in the concrete. We therefore find its application to the feelings and emotions, the daily tasks and the daily struggles of the individual man in the street easy and natural. So far from being a pure intellect or reason, the human being in the concrete may succeed by self-sophistication in convincing himself that his behaviour is always rational, but will never be treated on this basis by his friends and acquaintances, when they wish to forecast how he will act in certain given circumstances or to secure that he will act in a particular way. In our ordinary practical dealings with men we look not to the figures and moods of the syllogism for an explanation and understanding of their behaviour, but to what we know of their feelings, sentiments, and habits, their disposition and their character. This is precisely the attitude of the more recent psychology. The study of the inner forces of human nature, the active tendencies of man, has become the predominant characteristic of the psychology of the present day.

A man may do many things in the course of a single day. He gets out of bed in the morning, early it may be, washes and dresses, takes breakfast, works so many hours, takes other meals, smokes a cigarette or a pipe now and again, amuses himself in various ways, goes to bed at night and falls asleep to wake next morning and repeat essentially the same round of activities, though it may be details are altered. Now why does he do all these things, and at the time he does them ? It is not sufficient to say that so long as he is alive there must be activity of some sort. In this case we have activity of a particular sort and at a particular time, and in the mere fact of his being alive there is no reason why a man should be active in one way rather than another at any time. The man acts as he does because there is a motive prompting him to act in this particular way. In the motive we have the explanation of the act. In a sense it is the motive which acts.

When we seek the motives for the man's acts, we find that, however complex they may appear at first sight, they usually reduce themselves on analysis to certain motives more or less characteristic of human nature in general, though per-haps functioning in individual ways in particular individuals. Moreover, these motives are innate, that is, are part of the original nature and equipment of the human being. The human being comes into the world with certain active ten-dencies, derived primarily, we may say, from the life force itself, shaped and moulded through long evolutionary epochs into the several forms we find to-day. These active ten-dencies, so far as they are tendencies involving the co-opera-tion of experience in their working out, though independent of individual experience in their origin, may be designated instincts, the name by which they have been designated since the science of psychology came into being. These instincts are experienced as impulses, each accompanied by a feeling or interest, evoked by certain particular objects, situations, or other experiences, and manifesting themselves in more or less definite kinds of behaviour.

With these motive forces in view we can at once explain all the items of behaviour in our illustrative case. The man eats when and because he is hungry, apart from habits in virtue of which he eats at regular times, whether he is hungry or not. He goes to bed and sleeps when and because he feels the need of rest. He works in order to support himself and those dependent upon him, or, it may be, to acquire money and property in order to equal or surpass some one he desires to equal or surpass. And so the tale would run, referring always either to primary tendencies of human nature or other tendencies to action based upon such primary tendencies. Affection for parents, or children, or friends, love of wealth or power or social recognition, fear of death, uneasiness at isolation, anger against any one who injures or obstructs, and on a lower level hunger, thirst, and other natural or acquired appetites, desire of the pleasurable, aversion to the disagreeable—such is the nature of the motive forces we find operating in the conduct of the ordinary man, and of such nature are the forces which create, maintain, and underlie all social life.

The old and popular view that animals act by instinct and man in accordance with reason is very misleading. Instinct and reason or intelligence cannot be separated in this way. The relation of the two to one another may be best expressed, even in the case of the human being, by saying that instinct prescribes the end to be attained by our action, whereas intelligence finds the means of attaining that end. On the old view the chief psychological problem of human behaviour came to be to explain how it was possible for men sometimes to act unreasonably. The true psychological problem is to explain how they ever come to act reasonably.

The instinctive tendencies with which the human being starts in his life adventure arrange themselves in several well-marked groups. Perhaps the most important distinction is between the group of tendencies which, as it were, arise out of agreeable or disagreeable experiences, and those which take the form of reactions to situations, independently of previous agreeable or disagreeable experiences in connection with these situations. The first group of instinctive tendencies may be called appetitive, using the word in a wide signification which will include both appetite and aversion in the ordinary sense ; the second group, on the other hand, we may call 'reactive.' The appetitive tendencies originate, as it were, within us, in an affective experience we have, whereas the reactive tendencies are evoked by the apprehension of some object without or some situation in which we are placed. Appetitive tendencies are best represented in our well-marked appetites like hunger, thirst, sex, and the like. In all these cases certain 'uneasy sensations,' as some of the older psychologists put it, stimulate to action of a more or less definite kind to remove the 'uneasiness.' The 'reactive' tendencies are strikingly manifested among the lower animals in the behaviour accompanying fear and anger, and in the human being precisely the same phenomena may be encountered, though not perhaps on the same scale, or in the same simple uncomplicated form. Certain kinds of objects or situations evoke, even the first time they are met, a certain type of reaction. The child reacts to large animals displaying the signs of anger, or sudden and loud noises, or almost any sound in the dark, with the movements of flight and the emotion of fear, though it may never have previously had any disagreeable experiences either from an angry animal, or a situation characterized by a sudden and loud noise.

This distinction between appetitive tendencies and 'reactive' tendencies is a very important one, and is by no means confined to the instinct level. At higher levels we still have the distinction between tendencies to action springing from the agreeable or disagreeable in experience, and finding their end in simple feeling or emotion, and tendencies to action arising from fear, anger, self-display, and the like, and finding their end in some alteration in the external environment and its relation to the self, which will satisfy the underlying impulses.

At the lowest level the natural appetites, hunger, thirst, and the rest, arise in connexion with certain regularly recurring physical or physiological conditions. These conditions cause the kind of experience which the older psychologists called 'uneasiness,' and this in turn determines the craving we call the appetite. Obviously no account of human motives can be considered complete which fails to take note of these natural appetites and to recognize the peculiar insistence which is so characteristic of this type of motive force. But to the student of human nature, and to the social worker in particular, the acquired appetites, which may be taken to represent a somewhat higher level of development, are equally important and significant. Popularly we usually describe these acquired appetites as habits. We speak, for instance, of the drinking habit, the drug habit, the smoking habit. The social problems which various acquired appetites involve would be a great deal less complex and less serious if these could be reduced to habits and nothing more. We must recognize that the originating state of feeling and the craving which it determines are the essential elements to be taken into account.

At a higher stage of development still there are other acquired appetites of no small significance. Such acquired appetites may be based not only on sense pleasures of various kinds but on many forms of emotional excitement, even emotional excitement of a kind which at first is disagreeable, rather than the reverse, to the normal individual. In most of these cases the psychological evil and the social danger arise from the fact that the feeling, the normal function of which is to maintain and reinforce action so as to attain a definite end beyond, becomes for the appetite the end itself.

The part which emotion plays in the lives of different people illustrates admirably the difference between the appetitive and the reactive tendency at this level. The real and fundamental function of feeling and emotion, as we have just said, is to reinforce activity in pursuit of some end that is presumably of some utility—and ultimately of some biological utility —to the individual. Thus fear serves to reinforce the tendency to avoid and escape from any situation threatening the life or comfort of the individual or those in whom the individual is interested in the widest sense ; anger serves to reinforce the tendency to overcome any obstacles which resist

2

the development of the life—again in the widest sense.   And so of the other emotions.   In many individuals this is in the main the part that the emotions play.   In others, however—and these too are many—emotions themselves of practically all kinds come to be sought merely for the sake of the emotional experience.   An appetite for the emotion is developed, and the emotion no longer performs its function of reinforcing activity in pursuit of some end, but is itself the end.   People whom we call sentimentalists afford an admirable example of such phenomena.   They revel in emotional experiences of all kinds, passing from one emotional phase to another, and in most cases, except for the immediate acts and expressions, the emotions pass away without having effected any permanent result in the way of change in the environment, without any sustained activity even in pursuit of the appropriate end.

The emotional preacher is often surprised and disappointed at the slight permanent results achieved by what appear to him his happiest efforts.   The explanation is here.   Religious emotions are aroused, no doubt.   Some of the members of the congregation fairly riot in such emotions on the Sunday.   But these emotions evaporate without having fulfilled their proper function, partly because no opportunity is afforded for the appropriate actions.   On the Monday no trace remains except perhaps a craving for more excitement of the same kind, a craving which becomes stronger and stronger as the week goes on and next Sunday draws near, a craving also which is satisfied with greater and greater difficulty as Sunday succeeds Sunday.   The phenomena are indeed exactly parallel to phenomena which are clearly evident in the case of recognized acquired appetites on lower planes.[1]

Another distinction which is of considerable interest and importance is between those tendencies which are evoked by more or less specific objects, situations, or experiences, and which manifest themselves in more or less specific forms of behaviour, and those tendencies which are not evoked by

[1] This distinction between appetitive and reactive is a very old one, and constantly reappears in the history of psychology.   See for a very interesting discussion of the distinction, Plato's *Republic*, Bk. IV.

specific, but by many kinds of objects, situations, or experiences, and manifest themselves in all kinds of behaviour. The two groups may be designated specific tendencies, appetitive and reactive, and general tendencies, appetitive and reactive. Thus the tendency to escape is evoked by situations which may be labelled as 'dangerous,' the tendency to approach and investigate by situations which are novel and strange, and so on, while on the other hand the tendency to imitate may be evoked by all kinds of actions on the part of other people. Further, the escape tendency or curiosity manifests itself in a characteristic kind of behaviour, while imitation or play may manifest itself in all kinds of behaviour. The main general tendencies in the appetitive group are the tendency to seek and maintain the agreeable, and to avoid or cut short the disagreeable, in the reactive group the tendency to imitate the actions of others, the tendency to experience emotions in sympathy with others, and the play tendency.

Finally there are two groups of specific reactive tendencies which must be distinguished from one another. For this purpose the one group may be called the simple reactive tendencies, the other group the emotional reactive tendencies. The first play a great part in the early development of the child, the second in the whole life of both child and adult.

The earliest actions of the child are in most cases quite definite and specific responses to specific stimuli, and are the basis upon which are reared the most fundamental and important acquirements characteristic of the human being, complex co-ordinations of hand and hand, hand and foot, hand and eye, walking and running, speech, and the like. The enumeration of these simple reactive tendencies presents considerable difficulties. It is well-nigh impossible to say exactly where we pass over from the simple reflex—direct physiological response to stimulus without the intervention of any psychological factors—to the instinctive response depending on the co-operation of consciousness, and capable of modification and development because of this co-operation. But, although enumeration is difficult, classification

is possible.   The simple reactive tendencies may be classified
in four groups, according as the responses are directed towards
organ adjustment and attention, prehension, locomotion, or
vocalization.   Thus sucking, grasping after an object at a
distance, crawling, and babbling would illustrate the four
groups.

The emotional reactive tendencies demand somewhat more
detailed consideration.   Human reactive tendencies differ
from animal instincts in the fact that in the latter case a definite line of action is laid down for which provision is made
in the nervous structure, while in the former case, except for
the simple reactive tendencies, a definite line of action is not
laid down, but must be wrought out by the individual in the
course of his development and education.   In consequence
of this, and in order to secure the pursuing of lines of action
which are biologically necessary, the most important of the
reactive tendencies of the human being have associated with
them a strong emotional colouring.   Such emotional colouring we do not find to anything like the same extent in the
case of the lower animals, this difference becoming more and
more marked as we pass down the animal scale.   So striking
is this fact that McDougall has put forward the view, which
to some extent was held also by James and even older
psychologists, that human emotions can only be explained as
integral parts of human instincts.   Whether McDougall is
wholly right, or only partially right—he is certainly not wholly
wrong—this appears to be the most useful point of view from
which the student of human nature and the social student in
particular can approach the study of fundamental human
motives.

Looked at from McDougall's point of view, an emotional
reactive tendency presents the three aspects characteristic
of experience—knowing, feeling, and willing.   In the first
place it manifests itself in the apprehending of, and attending
to, objects or situations of a particular kind.   In the second
place it involves the experiencing in connexion with these
objects or situations of an emotion of a specific quality.   In
the third place it works itself out in acting or attempting

to act towards these objects or situations in a definite way.

The group of instinctive tendencies to which this description can apply includes the most important motive forces in human nature, apart from the appetites, as we have already indicated. An enumeration of the main tendencies belonging to the group would yield us : 1. The tendency to escape from danger, with its characteristic emotion fear. 2. The tendency of attack and active resistance, with its characteristic emotion anger. 3. The hunting tendency, with an emotion for which we have no specific name. 4. The gregarious tendency, with an emotion for which we again have no name. 5. The acquisitive tendency, with an emotion which becomes greed. 6. The inquisitive tendency, with an emotion which we call curiosity when present in relatively slight degree and wonder when strongly present. 7. The bipolar self tendency—towards self-display or towards self-abasement—with corresponding double emotion, called by McDougall, after Ribot, positive and negative self-feeling. 8. The tendency to protect offspring, with its emotion, for which in its simple form we have no name, but which we may call after McDougall tender emotion, or simply tenderness. These tendencies may be said to fall into two groups, the individual and the social, according as they are evoked under conditions which do not, or which do, involve a social reference. The latter constitute the instinctive basis of the social life of the human being, and would include the gregarious tendency, the acquisitive tendency, the self tendency, and the tendency to protect offspring—the parental instinct.

Most of these tendencies show themselves in the higher animals as well as in man. Based on a certain hereditary arrangement of nervous structure, developed in the course of race evolution, equally in man and in animals they determine primarily the objects to be sought or avoided, and the behaviour appropriate to objects of different kinds. Appearing in all men, yet they differ in their relative strength in different men, and such differences are the main basis of what we call differences of natural disposition, as distinct from differences of character. Most of them are capable of showing themselves in exaggerated form in various abnormal conditions, mainly conditions of the kind we group under the head of insanity. Serious defect in some of them may also bring an individual into the category of what we call the morally defective.

The question may perhaps be raised, why and how, from the biological point of view, the two types of reactive tendency have been developed, and what is the relation of the one type to the other. The answer is not difficult. The emotional tendencies may be regarded as representing what were originally series of simple responses following one another with definiteness and regularity, quite analogous to series of responses we still find in animal life, for example in the nest-building instincts of birds. The possibility of the adaptation to a complex and changing environment of such relatively definite series of specific reactions is obviously limited. Hence, in the course of evolutionary history the specific character of the individual responses, and the unvarying succession of the one response to the other have tended to disappear, and to be replaced by the emotional disturbance, which secures that those kinds of behaviour only that are effective towards the appropriate end, shall appeal to the organism. The consequences as regards development have been momentous. The emotion has come to be the permanent and abiding characteristic of the whole consciousness, while the particular kind of behaviour may be and is selected to meet the needs of the case, and this to a greater and greater extent as the scope of consciousness itself develops. In the human being these emotions —'primary emotions,' McDougall has called them—take rank among the most important of the motive forces constituting character and determining behaviour at all levels.

The extent to which these tendencies are capable of development and modification in the human being is practically unlimited, subject to one qualification. The accompanying emotion always retains its character, whatever else may be

changed. In all other respects the tendencies are highly
modifiable. They may come to be evoked by objects and
situations exceedingly remote from the objects and situations
which naturally evoke them ; they may issue in behaviour
utterly different from, and infinitely more complex than,
their crude natural behaviour.

The general method of ' transference ' of the instinctive
impulse from one object or situation to another is through
association. As a simple case of this let us consider a complex situation involving two objects A and B together. Let
us suppose that A is an object of the kind calculated to evoke
an instinctive tendency, say that of escape with the emotion
of fear. The situation accordingly, which we may call AB,
evokes fear. If the connexion of A and B is a frequent one,
in time B itself, through association, will come to evoke fear,
even when A, the original producing cause, is absent. This
may happen on the purely perceptual level ; that is, B may
evoke fear without the idea of A coming into consciousness
at all. It may happen on a far wider scale at the level we
call ideal representation, when the sentiment, which we shall
consider presently, is formed. At a higher level still, that
of thought proper, the most important kind of transference is
transference from the end to the means of attaining the end.
If there is a tendency towards an ideally represented end Y,
and it is realized that X is a necessary means towards
the attainment of Y, then the tendency attaches itself
in the first instance to X, and X is pursued with an intensity proportional to the strength of the tendency to seek
Y.

As regards behaviour, every rise in the scale of intelligence
involves increased possibility of its modification. At the
purely perceptual level successful kinds of activity become
fixed, unsuccessful disappear. The process of modification
or *learning* is immensely shortened if past experience can
be recalled in the form of idea, to guide the present action.
At the highest level of all—that of thought proper—the
seeing of relations, and the apprehending of different aspects
of a whole change the nature of the process altogether, for

the human being, conscious of a definite end in view, may seek out ways of attaining it, which will provide beforehand against practically every contingency in a way that the most perfect of animal instincts cannot approach.

NOTE.—There are many different classifications of human instincts. One of the most interesting of recent classifications is that of M. Larguier des Bancels. He founds on the attempt made by Descartes to give a biological classification, and he succeeds finally in enumerating the following groups : nutritional, protective, sexual, parental, social, egoistic, together with curiosity and play. At the recent International Congress of Psychology at Oxford Dr. Ernest Jones suggested a very interesting classification, partly biological and partly psychological. He first of all divided into two groups which may be termed ' attraction ' and ' repulsion ' respectively, and then subdivided into ' hunger ' and ' sexuality ' under the first head, and ' aversion,' ' flight,' and ' aggressiveness ' under the second.

CHAPTER IV

EMOTION, MOOD, AND SENTIMENT

EMOTIONS and sentiments represent the source of the engine power that drives human society, as habits and customs represent the flywheel. But emotions and sentiments are not independent sources of power. As we saw in the last chapter, the underlying motive forces in human life are manifested in the instinctive tendencies, and especially those with which the primary emotions are associated. Sentiments are merely a further development of the same motive forces, while the emotions we usually experience are either manifestations of these primary emotions themselves—fear, anger, curiosity, tenderness, and the like—or some combination of them more or less complex, with or without the organization due to the presence of a sentiment.

The psychological theory of the emotions is still in a somewhat backward state, but much has been done in recent times to clear up the actual facts. The main psychological difficulty is the relation of the emotions to the simple feelings. This difficulty has given rise to much controversy. The best way out of the difficulty appears to be to regard emotions as complex phenomena of experience, constituted by a mass of organic sensations, definite impulses, and simple feelings, all combined in the total mental state. At all events, a well-marked emotional experience always involves a number of physiological reactions, which affect consciousness to a greater or less extent—the so-called 'organic resonance'—an impulsive force, which in intense emotions may suspend the higher mental processes and "overwhelm purposes, resolutions, and principles by its irresistible urgency towards immediate action," a narrowing and specializing of consciousness, and a pronounced feeling tone. Moreover, as regards feeling tone, the primary emotions always exhibit that bipolarity which is so characteristic of feeling—pleasure—unpleasure, satisfaction—dissatisfaction—and the organic resonance also seems in some measure to vary accordingly. Joy and sorrow are not individual emotions but opposite characters of all the primary emotions. Thus we have the joy of tenderness, the joy of self-glorification, the joy of acquisition, the joy of battle, the joy of escape from danger, the sorrow of tenderness, the sorrow of humiliation and defeat, the sorrow of deprivation or loss, the sorrow of baffled rage, the sorrow of despairing efforts to escape. All the joys when intense or acute find vent in laughter, as the sorrows may find vent in tears.

Many of the physiological reactions are matters of every-day experience. Changes in the rate of the heart-beat, flushing or paling of the face, disturbance of the breathing, sweating, trembling of the limbs—all these are well-known symptoms and expressions of emotion. But recent investigations have brought to light many other curious physiological changes, some of which have far-reaching importance. Such are the phenomena of digestion, studied by Pavlov and his co-workers in Russia, and by Cannon and others in America. Pavlov found that while under normal conditions the sight of food or any sign previously associated with food would call forth in the hungry dog secretion of saliva and gastric juice—the 'appetite' juice—under the influence of pain, fear, or anger this secretion was inhibited. Cannon similarly found that the digestive movements of the stomach and intestines were inhibited by anger or distress.

The results of these investigations are so important that we may quote Cannon's statement of the findings at length : "Hornborg found that when the boy whom he studied chewed agreeable food a more or less active secretion of the gastric juice was started, whereas the chewing of indifferent material was without influence. Not only is it true that normal secretion is favoured by pleasurable sensations during mastication but also that unpleasant feelings, such as vexation and some of the major emotions, are accompanied by a failure of secretion. Thus Hornborg was unable to confirm in his patient the observation of Pawlow that mere sight of food to a hungry subject causes the flow of gastric juice. Hornborg explains the difference between his and Pawlow's results by the difference in the reaction of the subjects to the situation. When food was shown, but withheld, Pawlow's hungry dogs were all eagerness to secure it, and the juice at once began to flow. Hornborg's little boy, on the contrary, became vexed when he could not eat at once, and began to cry; then no secretion appeared. Bogen also reports that his patient, a child, aged three and a half years, sometimes fell into such a passion in consequence of vain hoping for food, that the giving of the food, after calming the child, was not followed by any secretion of the gastric juice.

" The observations of Bickel and Sasaki confirm and define more precisely the inhibitory effects of violent emotion on gastric secretion. They studied these effects on a dog, with an œsophageal fistula, and with a side pouch of the stomach which, according to Pawlow's method, opened only to the exterior. If the animal was permitted to eat while the œsophageal fistula was open the food passed out through the fistula and did not go to the stomach. Bickel and Sasaki confirmed the observation of Pawlow that this sham feeding is attended by a copious flow of gastric juice, a true ' psychic secretion,' resulting from the pleasurable taste of the food. In a typical instance the sham feeding lasted five minutes, and the secretion continued for twenty minutes, during which time 66·7 c.c. of pure gastric juice was produced.

" On another day a cat was brought into the presence of the dog, whereupon the dog flew into a great fury. The cat was soon removed, and the dog pacified. Now the dog was again given the sham feeding for five minutes. In spite of the fact that the animal was hungry and ate eagerly, there was no secretion worthy of mention.   During a period of twenty minutes, corresponding to the previous observation, only 9 c.c. of acid fluid was produced, and this was rich in mucus.   It is evident that in the dog, as in the boy observed by Bogen, strong emotions can so profoundly disarrange the mechanisms of secretion that the natural nervous excitation accompanying the taking of food cannot cause the normal flow.

" On another occasion Bickel and Sasaki started gastric secretion in the dog by sham feeding, and when the flow of gastric juice had reached a certain height the dog was infuriated for five minutes by the presence of the cat.   During the next fifteen minutes there appeared only a few drops of a very mucous secretion.   Evidently in this case a physiological process, started as an accompaniment of a psychic state quietly pleasurable in character, was almost entirely stopped by another psychic state violent in character.

" It is noteworthy that in both the positive and negative results of the emotional excitement illustrated in Bickel and Sasaki's dog the effects persisted long after the removal of the exciting condition.   This fact Bickel was able to confirm in a girl with œsophageal and gastric fistulas ; the gastric secretion long outlasted the period of eating, although no food entered the stomach.   The importance of these observations to personal economics is too obvious to require elaboration.

" Not only are the secretory activities of the stomach unfavourably affected by strong emotions ; the movements of the stomach as well, and indeed the movements of almost the entire alimentary canal, are wholly stopped during excitement." [1]

As Cannon says, the moral is too obvious to require drawing. In addition to these phenomena, changes in the composition

---

[1] Quoted from Morton Prince, " The Unconscious."   Cf. Cannon, W. B.,   " Bodily Changes in Pain, Hunger, Fear and Rage," p. 8 et seq.

of the blood, leading, for example, in the case of anger, to greater coagulability, in the electrical condition of the body, in the state of the muscular system, and so on, have been demonstrated. So extensive may the physiological disturbance become in the case of frequently recurring emotions—and fear or anxiety is the emotion which is more particularly apt to show this result—that the feeling element is itself masked, and the physiological disturbances, in the absence of this explanation of their source, are regarded and treated, even by medical men, as symptomatic of disease of the heart, the stomach, or the nervous system.

The most interesting of the psychical effects of emotion is probably the narrowing and specializing of consciousness. When under the influence of a strong emotion we may become blind and deaf to everything which is not relevant to the end determined by the emotion ; we may forget principles and resolutions ; we may even temporarily break away from what might be described as characteristically the whole trend of our life activity. In all these cases the psychological process known as ' dissociation ' is involved, and some kind and degree of emotional dissociation is a matter of everyday experience. This is more than the mere regulative function of feeling. It is a definite blocking of those connecting paths in the nervous system—and in the mind—which normally ensure the due balance and control of our various interests and activities. In extreme cases an individual may lose control of fundamental muscular and sensory mechanisms. Speech may be lost, and the control of still earlier and more primitive functions and co-ordinations may disappear. Usually this dissociation is merely temporary, and normal conditions are restored as the emotion passes away. Occasionally, however, more or less permanent dissociations may take place, when the case becomes distinctly pathological. Numerous instances of such pathological dissociation occurred during the war, and in their various forms were all popularly included under the designation ' shell-shock.'

A mood may be defined as a condition showing emotional

phenomena in the state a physiologist would call 'sub-excitation.' There is no actual experience of emotion, but some of the processes involved in a particular emotion are in a certain degree active in such a way as to facilitate the development of that emotion. Organic changes, involved it may be in the general state of health at the time, or arising directly or indirectly from mental causes beneath the threshold of clear personal consciousness, may give a general tone to all experience. Or an emotional disturbance may be just subsiding, and, though the experience is no longer emotional, organic changes are still going on as a result of the emotion, which as before give a tone to the whole experience at the moment. In either case we have a mood present. The characteristic of a mood is the facility with which emotional disturbance may be produced. An individual is in an irritable mood, let us say. An incident, which would ordinarily only provoke a smile, now evokes perhaps violent anger. There is a tendency for a mood to fasten upon anything and everything as an exciting cause for the development of the emotion.

We must distinguish a mood from a sentiment. Both are conditions which determine or modify experience rather than themselves experiences, but a mood is a relatively transitory, a sentiment a relatively permanent condition—a disposition. McDougall, following Shand, has defined a sentiment as " an organized system of emotional tendencies centred about some object." The definition is a useful one, but it ought to be added that the organized system may consist of a single emotional tendency, and that, in the human being at least, it is the idea of the object rather than the object itself with which it is associated. In consequence of the existence of a sentiment the presence in consciousness of the idea of the object imparts to the consciousness as a whole an emotional colouring, and may make it distinctly emotional with one or other of the associated emotions according to the circumstances of the case. The general result of the development of sentiment is that the being— human or animal—comes to possess what we call character rather than natural disposition. To this point we shall return presently.

Sentiments may be simple or they may be exceedingly complex. The simplest of all sentiments is formed when a single emotional tendency is associated with the idea of a particular object. For example, we may have had some terrifying experience in connexion with a certain object—animal, person, place—as a result of which the idea of that object cannot rise in consciousness without some reawakening of the emotion. A sentiment has therefore been formed. A simple sentiment of this type may become complex in either of two ways. The idea with which the emotional tendency or ' affect ' is associated may itself have, or acquire, associations with other ideas, and carry its affect with it into the idea complexes to which it belongs. Or, since an emotional disturbance of practically any kind renders the individual while it lasts peculiarly liable to certain other kinds of emotional disturbance, other emotional tendencies may come to be evoked by, and associated with, the original object, sc that a sentiment which is complex on the emotion side is developed. Development of the simple into the complex usually takes place in both ways.

The typical sentiments of ordinary life are love and hate. Both are complex sentiments on the emotion side, in that a variety of different emotions may in either case be evoked according to the circumstances in which the object of the sentiment is placed. Thus, in the case of love, fear on account of the object, anger at anything injuring the object, tenderness, pride, humiliation, and so on, may all be evoked, and the same kind of thing is true of hate. The development of both from simple sentiments can often be traced. Thus hate for an individual might easily develop from such a simple fear sentiment as we have already described. In both cases also complication on the idea side can often be traced. For example, hate of an individual may develop into hate of all individuals belonging to the same social class, town, or nationality. Love of a particular dog may readily become love of dogs in general, of all animals, of the abstract quality of kindness to animals, and so on.

Of the same order as the sentiments are the complex acquired interests. They differ from the sentiments merely in the fact that emotional disturbance is absent or relatively slight, but there is probably no sharp line of demarcation. A personal value becomes attached to certain objects or pursuits, and the personal value, though it does not as a rule give rise to anything of the nature of emotion, is nevertheless rooted in feeling. Like the sentiments, the interests contribute to the formation of what we call the character of an individual. " Tell me what you like, and I'll tell you what you are," says Ruskin. That an individual's interests are a good index to his character is universally recognized. But interests are more than an index to character. They are constituent elements in character.

The mode in which interests and sentiments function in our lives can be indicated briefly, but would require a volume for detailed description. When at any time two emotional tendencies are operating simultaneously the outcome in behaviour will depend on the tendencies in question and their relation to one another. If the two tendencies are capable of existing together, the behaviour will be a complication of the behaviours appropriate to each, any difference in strength between the tendencies, or in intensity between the emotions, showing itself by an emphasizing of the corresponding elements in the combined behaviour. If, on the contrary, the two emotional tendencies are incapable of existing together, or practically so, as when one tendency prompts towards behaviour of a kind antagonistic to, or inconsistent with, the behaviour to which the other tendency prompts, conflict must arise, and the conflict will only be resolved when the stronger tendency succeeds in temporarily repressing the other and translating itself into action. The temporary repression may be only of the nature of suspension or postponement, so that when the stronger tendency has achieved its end or satisfaction, and disappears, the weaker tendency, if the situation is still such as to evoke it, dominates consciousness in its turn and achieves its end.

While we have to do merely with the instinctive tendencies and the primary emotions, there will obviously be a continual succession of evoked tendencies, fusions, conflicts, repressions, suspensions, without any stability in the inner life or consistency in the behaviour. The succession of knowings, feelings, and strivings, making up the inner life, is determined on the one hand by the original nature of the individual, manifesting itself in his appetites and reactive tendencies, on the other hand by external objects, to which the individual reacts ; and, as every change in the environment will evoke new impulses, the inner life will be a " mere chaos, without order, consistency, or continuity of any kind." The behaviour, which is the outcome of this inner life, will be similarly inconsistent and chaotic.

As soon as sentiments and interests come upon the scene a measure of stability and consistency is introduced, and a new phase of development begins. If character means essentially and fundamentally that quality, or those qualities, of an individual's ' make-up,' which, if known, enable us in some degree to foresee and predict how he will act and continue to act in various given situations, then obviously, as we have already indicated, the development of sentiments and interests marks the beginning of the development of character. Psychology has of course nothing to do with the moral valuation of characters. For psychology character is simply a psychical fact. As a psychical fact character implies a stability which natural tendencies, functioning on the instinctive level, can never possess. For in such a case, as we have shown, behaviour must necessarily be determined by the immediate environment. Stability will be secured when instinctive tendencies can be consistently inhibited, or modified in a certain direction, no matter what the immediate environment may be, which can only happen when the instinctive tendencies evoked come into conflict, not with one another, but with emotional tendencies belonging to a permanent inner system, the activity of which is relatively

3

independent of the immediate environment.   The sentiment or interest is precisely such an inner system.

The processes involved in conflicts, in which sentiments are participants, are enormously important.   James has stated a law of the instinctive level, which he calls the " law of inhibition by habit."   Strictly there is no such law, or rather, James' statement of his law sums up very inade-quately the facts it is meant to cover, which are the very facts we are at present considering.   For ' habit ' we ought to read ' sentiment.'   Conflict between instinctive tendency and sentiment—and also conflict between sentiment and sentiment, which James does not appear to contemplate at all in the formulation of the law—is in an entirely different category from conflict between one instinctive tendency and another, and the phenomena of this higher type of conflict seem certainly to demand the formulation of a new and special law, but these phenomena are much more complex than James' law would indicate.   Perhaps the general law might be formulated in some such terms as these : Where an instinct-ive tendency comes into conflict with a sentiment, or one sentiment comes into conflict with another sentiment, one of three results may emerge according to circumstances : (a) successful and total repression, (b) imperfect repression, with recurring conflicts, and often dissociation and abnormal manifestations of various kinds, (c) sublimation.

When the sentiment is powerful and pervasive, and the emotional tendency is not of the very highest intensity, the first result may be produced.   Where the sentiment is not so powerful and the emotional tendency is on the con-trary powerful, or generally, when the sentiment is unable permanently to repress the tendency, the second result may be produced, and no real solution of the conflict takes place.   Where both are powerful, and neverthe-less a solution of the conflict is found, this solution is by way of sublimation.   That is to say, the tendency operates, but in a manner so as to harmonize with the sentiment.

This ground has been very carefully worked over by Freud

and his followers, and the psychologist, even while refusing to accept many of the Freudian theories and interpretations, may well acknowledge the debt psychology owes to Freud for the industry and perspicuity with which this obscure and yet highly important part of our complex nature has been explored, and made to yield up facts of the utmost significance for the understanding of human conduct. Readers who desire a full discussion of this topic and the facts upon which Freudian theories are based cannot do better than consult Freudian works. All that can be attempted here is to get the main points clear, and a particular illustrative case will best serve this purpose.

Let us take the sex instinct with its emotional accompaniments. Under the conditions of modern civilized life this instinct necessarily comes into conflict with practically the whole mass of sentiments representing civilization in the individual mind. At least there is usually a period in each individual life, during which this is the case. What takes place ? Repression may be completely successful, at any rate as far as the observable life of the individual, inner and outer, is concerned. We refrain from attempting to estimate the proportion of cases in which this solution of the conflict is found. It is certainly not the usual solution. The usual solution is sublimation. The energy belonging to the sex instinct is drafted into lines of activity which are in harmony with the more pervasive sentiments, and which may even develop within, and as it were under the protection of, a sentiment. These lines of activity may possibly have a close relation to, but more often have a very remote connexion with, the natural lines of activity of the instinct. Pursuits are followed and ends are sought with an energy the source of which is an entire mystery apart from the underlying sex instinct. Where solution of the conflict is not reached, or only imperfectly reached, phenomena which are morbid or pathological in various degrees manifest themselves, which need not detain us here.

What is true of the sex instinct is also true of the other instinctive tendencies. We should, however, expect to find

that the phenomena arising in connexion with conflict
between an instinctive tendency and a sentiment exhibit
degrees of prominence and pervasiveness in keeping with
the pervasiveness and strength of the tendencies and sentiments involved. The more fundamental, the more powerful,
the more insistent in its demands the instinctive tendency,
the more difficult is the solution of the conflict by repression.
Hence we should expect to find the sex instinct playing
something like the part assigned to it by Freud, but hardly
that it would be the only tendency playing such a part, in
determining various abnormalities and disturbances having
a mental origin, which are undoubtedly very characteristic
of modern civilized life.

We cannot leave the topic of the sentiments without taking
some notice of the most important sentiment of all, the self
sentiment, called by McDougall the 'self-regarding sentiment.' This is the sentiment upon which the stability of
the inner life as a whole almost entirely depends, and which
gives the personality such organization as it possesses at this
level. While every sentiment that is formed makes for
stability in a certain special direction, the self sentiment
makes for stability in all social relations, and at the same
time by, as it were, joining up all the other sentiments gives
stability to the whole.

As soon as the idea of the self develops, the self tendencies,
positive and negative, become associated with it, and the self
sentiment is formed. The idea of self developed is always
the idea of a social self. It is the idea, as McDougall has
pointed out, not merely of the individual's body, and of
bodily and mental functions, but of a system of relations
between the individual and other individuals. The result is
that the individual comes to see himself in the light of the
opinions and feelings of others with respect to him. Hence,
if the development of the self sentiment is normal, its influence
in shaping the individual into a member of society is not
difficult to understand. The feeling of inferiority, which the
recognition of the superiority of others involves, may come
as a very disagreeable experience when it is forced upon the

individual by the disapproval of other people, which he incurs by acting in a certain way, while an agreeable experience, in the shape of positive self feeling, will result from the approval of other people, and will stimulate those ways of acting which have secured such a result. Further, isolation, being boycotted or sent to Coventry, is a very disagreeable experience to most individuals, because man is essentially a social being through the operation both of the gregarious instinct and of the self tendencies. Hence public opinion can in various ways exercise a powerful influence in shaping the conduct and development of the individual through the activity of the self sentiment.

It ought to be particularly emphasized that the development of the self sentiment must be normal if normal results are to be produced. If the feeling of inferiority is constantly evoked the result is usually the development of some defence mechanism or other, in which the self seeks security or protection in the give and take of social life, and some defence mechanisms greatly modify the whole situation, as we shall see later.[1] If the feeling of superiority is constantly evoked, and the feeling of inferiority never, as with a child that has every wish gratified, that never has any authority exercised over it, that never meets with opposition, or prohibition, or blame, we may have the development of a pride, that knows no humility, can feel no shame, and responds to disapproval simply with anger at the obstruction to the gratification of the self tendency. It is obvious that in either case the control over behaviour exercised by the self sentiment would be warped and from the social point of view distorted. The individual must have a sense of his own value, a healthy tendency to enjoy the approving or admiring regards of others, and to find humiliation in the eyes of others intensely disagreeable; but he must also be capable of shame.

Let us consider finally in what sense the self sentiment can be said to organize the whole inner life. McDougall has

---

[1] See Chapter VII.

shown very clearly that the self of the self sentiment tends to expand so as to include much that is not strictly speaking the self at all. The process is entirely a social process, and the general law under which the phenomena may be brought might be expressed thus : Whenever the personal reactions of other people towards any individual are determined or modified by the connexion, accidental or otherwise, of that individual with some other object of their favourable or unfavourable regard, that object tends so far to become part of the idea of self, forming the nucleus of the self sentiment. Any particular expansion of the self in accordance with this law may be merely temporary, or permanent but only occasional, or permanent and relatively constant. The family, club, church, town, or nationality to which we belong may illustrate this expansion. In all cases it involves the merging of any particular sentiments represented by these objects in the self sentiment.

Seeing that opinions, beliefs, sentiments, conduct are so very frequently the objects of the approving or disapproving regard of others, these, so far as they are personally recognized as characteristic of us, become also, as it were, caught up into the self sentiment. Moreover, all sentiments whatsoever, so far as they represent what might be termed personal values, belong to the self of the self sentiment and their objects tend not only to evoke the emotions of the particular sentiment itself, but also call into activity the self sentiment, and tend to evoke its emotions.

The general result is that the whole inner life becomes organized with the self sentiment forming what might be called the core or centre, and the other sentiments arranged in relation to it in their order of relative dominance. McDougall has pointed out that the arrangement is in the nature of a hierarchy, with one sentiment—the master sentiment— at the top. In normal cases this view must be modified by taking into consideration the all-pervasive influence of the self sentiment. It is really the self sentiment which gives the master sentiment its dominant position. But there may be a hierarchy, and a master sentiment, independently of the self sentiment, where the latter is weak or practically absent altogether. We must perhaps consider all such cases as abnormal, but they are fairly numerous nevertheless. The lover, the fanatic, the miser may serve as types.

NOTE.—The term 'complex' has come to be a recognized term in recent psychology, owing in the main to the influence of Freudian writers. There is still some dispute about the exact sense in which it ought to be used, but generally speaking its meaning is very similar to the meaning we have given to 'sentiment.' The main point to be noted is that it is usually employed of a repressed feeling system. Repressed complexes are not always wholly 'unconscious,' as Freudian psychologists seem to imply. Nevertheless there is undoubtedly evidence that there are such unconscious complexes, and there is strong presumptive evidence that there are factors in the makeup of an individual, of the same nature and type as the complex, but belonging to a level of life below, or dating from a stage of development anterior to, the level or stage of conscious process as we generally understand it.

CHAPTER V

SOCIAL INTERACTION

W E have already shown that some of the emotional reactive tendencies are of very great social importance, in that they determine the individual's behaviour with regard to other individuals in various ways. This is particularly the case with the gregarious instinct and the self tendency, which may be said to underlie social life, as well as the protective or parental instinct which makes the development of higher types of social life possible. But there are other reactive tendencies which are of equal social importance, as avenues by means of which social influence makes itself felt in the development of the individual. These are the tendency to imitate in the sphere of behaviour, the tendency to experience emotion sympathetically in the sphere of feeling, and the tendency to accept suggestions in the sphere of opinion and belief. These tendencies, imitation, sympathy, and suggestibility, differ from those we have already considered, in that they are not evoked by any specific kind of situation, in that they do not involve in their activity any specific feeling or emotion, and in that they do not issue in behaviour of a particular kind. They are general, not specific, reactive tendencies.

All these tendencies are closely related to one another, so that they might all be regarded as manifestations of a single tendency, which might be called imitation, in a wide sense. Or they might all be regarded as appendages of the gregarious instinct, modes in which the gregarious instinct manifests itself. The objection to the first way of regarding them is that psychologically they are quite distinct from one another, however difficult it may be to distinguish their respective outcomes in act. The objection to the second is that, though closely related to the gregarious instinct, they are similarly psychologically quite distinct from it. The gregarious instinct may bring the crowd together, and help to hold it together. In the crowd we may experience the emotion of the gregarious instinct in the joy of bathing, as it were, in the crowd effect. But this is a different thing from the imitation or sympathy which the operation of the gregarious instinct renders possible.

We shall probably understand the situation best by an attempt to define the three tendencies. Imitation is the tendency to act as we see others acting. Sympathy is the tendency to experience a feeling or emotion on perceiving the expressive signs of that feeling or emotion in another. Suggestibility is more difficult to define. Nor is its status among the various human tendencies at all clear. Tentatively we may define it as the tendency to accept uncritically and act upon ideas, beliefs, and opinions, expressed in the words, attitudes, or acts of other people.

We may begin with imitation. We realize very imperfectly the part which imitation plays in ordinary life, so long as we confine our attention to the mere external fact that one individual repeats the acts of another, without inquiring into all that this involves. The mere repetition of actions is in itself of relatively little significance. The important thing is that imitation is, on the one hand, a method of learning to do things, on the other hand, the means by which very important kinds of knowledge are acquired. To a large extent the lower animals have definite lines of action laid down for them beforehand, and provision made for these lines of action in the structure and arrangement of their nervous systems ; man has to lay down lines of action for himself, and has to learn to do many things the lower animals can do without learning. This indicates the main biological function of imitation. The ends of action may be prescribed by the specific instinctive tendencies, but the means of attaining these ends must be learned, and the learning takes

place very largely by way of imitation. All the animals
of the same species behave in practically the same way, and
with less flexibility the lower down the animal scale. The
same end result may be reached in the case of the human
being, but with the addition of infinitely greater flexibility,
because the human being has to learn through imitation.

We must distinguish the different levels at which imitation
may take place. At the first or lowest level there is instinctive or unconscious imitation, the kind of imitation by which
we unconsciously acquire tricks of speech and gesture, that
may stay with us to the end as witnesses of the social environment in which we developed. In these flexibility is at its
minimum as far as the human being is concerned. At the
highest level there is purposive or deliberate imitation, when
we imitate either because we wish to learn to perform the
action, or because we desire that to which the action leads.
Here flexibility is at its maximum, and there is room for
originality, inventiveness, and, from the social point of view,
progress. Midway between the two extremes, in respect of
flexibility and in respect of value, is that imitation in which
we neither copy directly and unconsciously from the act,
nor deliberately with reference to an end we have in view,
but from an idea of the act which we have in our own minds,
and because of some kind of interest in the act which is
merely temporary.

The knowledge we acquire through imitation is of very
great importance. For one thing it is evident we acquire
knowledge of our own powers and limitations ; but that is
only a part of the story. We learn to know ourselves, not
merely as individuals, but as members of society, and we learn
to know society as composed of individuals like ourselves.
The growth of self-consciousness in the human being takes
place largely through imitation, and is very largely a social
process. Baldwin[1] has described the process in detail. He
distinguishes three stages in the development of our knowledge of society and of ourselves as members of society.
These stages he calls the ' projective,' ' subjective,' and

[1] "Mental Development in the Child and the Race."

' ejective ' stages. According to this account the child's attention is first drawn to other persons in his environment in contradistinction to things, because of the irregularity, capriciousness, unpredictable character of their reactions. This first stage of the arousing of special interest in other persons and their actions is the ' projective ' stage. Persons are merely separated from inanimate things as specially interesting, but capricious, and ' ununderstandable ' elements in the environment. But this special interest in the behaviour of other persons involves a special stimulus to imitate their behaviour, and by imitating the acts of other persons the child learns in his own experience how these acts feel and what they mean. This is the subjective stage. It puts the child in a position to interpret the behaviour of other people from his own experience, and when he knows and interprets others from, and in terms of, what he feels in himself, he has reached the ' ejective ' stage. In order to understand other people he simply ejects his own experience when he acts as they are acting. Hence, as we have already had occasion to point out, the self-consciousness of the developed human being is consciousness of a social self, because the individual knows himself through others, and others through himself and both in relation to one another, the knowledge having been acquired through, and by virtue of, imitation of the behaviour of others.

Educationists and practical social workers are more particularly interested in imitation as underlying the influence of example. It is of some importance to know the main conditions under which the force of example is felt, and the main psychological question is whether an individual tends as a rule to imitate his equals or his superiors. Without going into unnecessary details we may answer the question gener-ally by saying that, as regards unconscious imitation, the fact of superiority is of relatively small significance, and frequency of association is the main consideration; but so far as other forms of imitation are concerned, an individual tends to imitate his superiors, rather than his equals or inferiors, yet not those who are superior to such an extent as to inhibit all attempt at imitation. A feeling of inferiority puts the individual into a receptive attitude in this and in other respects, if the feeling of inferiority is not too intense, or the inferiority itself not too great.

Sympathy, the second of the tendencies, need not detain us long. Through sympathy we come to experience the feelings and emotions of those with whom we come into contact, even more or less accidental contact. The stimulating cause of the feeling or emotion appears to be the apprehending of its natural expressive signs. Illustrations are so numerous that we need hardly spend time on them. Curiosity and fear especially are notoriously contagious. The spread of panic is an illustration of the second. Any one who stops suddenly in the street, and gazes upwards, may have any day a striking illustration of the first. Sympathy plays a great part in the psychology of crowds, and both actor and orator rely on it very largely for their effects. Its more permanent results are to be seen in the community of feeling and sentiment characteristic of individuals belonging to definite groups, members of the same family, the same church, the same club.

There seems to be no doubt as to the instinctive nature of sympathy. In the presence of the natural expressive signs of an emotion, we tend to experience the emotion, even although we have never experienced it before, provided it is an emotion we are capable of experiencing. In this fact we have a possible explanation of at least some of the reported manifestations of instinctive behaviour with respect to particular objects and situations, on the part of children, and a warning as to our own manifestations of emotion in the presence of children. In the development of the human being it plays an important part in two directions. On the one hand, through the sympathetic induction of emotion, an understanding of the feelings and actions of other people is developed. On the other hand, through sympathy the child's emotional attitudes assimilate themselves to the emotional attitudes of his social *milieu* and develop as his environment expands.

Suggestion and suggestibility must be considered in some-what more detail. To begin with it is well to remember that the psychologist uses the word ' suggestion ' in a special-ized and technical sense, which is not the sense of popular speech. In our ordinary speech anything in our experience which signifies or points to something else, or recalls something to memory, is said to suggest that other thing. In psychology to ' suggest ' means to convey opinions, beliefs, and ideas, and to influence behaviour, in a characteristic way and under special conditions. Suggestion always implies personal interaction between two individuals.[1] It is a way in which personal influence makes itself felt. It is, in fact, that particular method of exerting personal influence by which one individual is brought to accept from another a statement, opinion, or belief, and to act upon it, without having, or seeking to have, adequate logical grounds for its acceptance.

Some of the phenomena of suggestion were recognized long ago and were classed with the phenomena of sympathy and imitation. But a careful study of the phenomena of suggestion as such was first made in connexion with the study of hypnotism. Exaggerated suggestibility is one of the most characteristic symptoms of the hypnotic condition. To such an extent is this the case that the condition has been defined as a condition of exaggerated suggestibility artificially induced. In the hypnotic condition the patient or subject is to a large, but varying, extent at the mercy of suggestions coming from the hypnotist. His beliefs and opinions are controlled even in conditions of light hypnosis; in deeper hypnosis even his perceptions may be controlled, so that hallucinations, both positive and negative, may be readily induced. However marvellous the phenomena of hypnotism may appear, it is necessary to remember that analogous phenomena occur when there is no question of hypnotism at all, and most of the phenomena have analogues more or less close in our normal, waking, everyday life.

[1] The phenomena of auto-suggestion— ' self-suggestion ' —would seem to be inconsistent with this statement. The underlying prin-ciple, however, could easily be extended so as to cover these phenomena.

In particular this is true of phenomena which depend upon suggestion.

The general condition upon which suggestion depends may be best described by saying that, when any idea presents itself in our consciousness, which involves believing or acting in a certain way, any factors which prevent opposing ideas rising in consciousness will tend to make us believe or act in accordance with the idea presented, and so far therefore make us suggestible. The extent to which opposing ideas can be prevented from rising in consciousness will be a measure of suggestibility. This prevention of the rise of opposing ideas is of the nature of dissociation, which we have already met with as a characteristic phenomenon of emotion. Suggestion might therefore be described as a means of producing dissociation, and suggestibility as the tendency for dissociation phenomena to manifest themselves under certain special conditions.

The general tendency will be better understood if we consider a few simple instances of its operation, or otherwise. When one says at table : " Please pass the sugar," immediately, and without any consciousness of the request as a request, hands are extended. But suppose it is the dinner table, and no sugar is required for the course, or there is no sugar on the table, the tendency to carry out the idea of action may be experienced, but it will be immediately checked by the other circumstances of the situation. Or better, suppose, in place of making such a simple request, one should say : " Please jump out of the window." The tendency to do the action would be present as before, but for so brief an instant as almost to escape notice, the associations called up, as the significance of the words becomes clear, sufficing at once to inhibit any such tendency. In cases of high suggestibility, however, as for example in the hypnotic condition, even an idea like this might act itself out.

Another example will illustrate another aspect of the process. If some one says : " Don't smile," or " Don't yawn," or " Don't spell accommodate with one 'm,' " the tendency is as a rule to do what has been forbidden. It is not at first clear how this can be reconciled with our account of suggestion, or with the other examples just given of its operation. The fact is the suggestive value of ' don't ' is always slight and usually negative, because it does not bring into an individual's mind any idea of action, but the idea of inhibiting action, and the idea of the action must first be present. Accordingly the positive suggestions in the ideas of the respective actions will be present to begin with, and may even to the end prove stronger than the suggestion of the ' don't.'

One more example. Suppose some one says confidently and with conviction : " There is only one ' m ' in accommodate," the effect of the statement, as regards carrying belief, will depend on the audience to whom it is made. If they are school children and the speaker is their teacher, they will probably accept the statement without hesitation. So also may an audience ignorant of the spelling of the word, or not certain about it, provided they regard the speaker as likely to know the correct spelling. On the other hand an audience composed of individuals who are quite familiar with the correct spelling of the word, will in general—though there may be many exceptions—refuse to accept the statement. In the last case the tendency to accept may be momentarily present, but the idea of ' spelling accommodate,' itself a definite and established idea of action, overpowers the suggestion to misspell.

Hence conditions which favour suggestion are in the main conditions which, directly or indirectly, inhibit opposing ideas. Such conditions can be classified. First of all they are divisible into two main groups, subjective and objective conditions depending on the personal characteristics, temporary or permanent, of the individual receiving the suggestion, and conditions depending on something external to him. The latter are further divisible into : (1) conditions affecting the source from which the suggestion comes, (2) conditions affecting the circumstances in which it comes, and (8) conditions affecting the manner in which it is given.

As regards the subjective conditions, they are somewhat easily specified. The non-appearance of opposing ideas may be due to the lack of such ideas, dependent either on youth and consequent lack of experience, or on lack of knowledge in connexion with the topic under discussion when the suggestion is given. Or the failure of opposing ideas to rise in consciousness may be due to inhibition through dissociation, which would imply the presence of one or other of a number of more or less abnormal conditions, of which fatigue, sickness, hysteria, and hypnosis are the chief. Or finally, opposing ideas may be inhibited by individual characteristics like lack of self-confidence, a feeling of inferiority, and so on. These individual peculiarities may be merely temporary or relatively permanent in character, and tend to produce all degrees of suggestibility.

The objective conditions demand more careful attention. As we have said there are three groups of such conditions. The first group consists of the conditions affecting the source from which the suggestion comes. The general principle upon which they all depend is that anything which gives the source what we call *prestige* will favour suggestion emanating from that source. This indicates the important part which the self tendency plays in the commoner forms of suggestion. Two kinds of prestige may be distinguished. In the first place there is individual prestige, that is the prestige which belongs to an individual. Such prestige may be personal— that is, it may arise from an individual's personality, his force of character, his strength of will, or his personal fascination, perhaps—or it may be derived or acquired—that is, it may be due to more or less accidental attributes, such as wealth, position, reputation, good family, fine clothes, a uniform, and the like. Every gathering, crowd, set, or clique has its leader, and leadership depends on this individual prestige. In the second place there is mass prestige, the prestige of numbers, or it may be of custom or tradition. All kinds of effects in everyday life, and more especially perhaps in politics or in religion, may be traced to this kind of prestige. It is not mere daring that is required to stand alone in any belief, or any course of action ; it requires also strength of character, confidence in one's self, if the suggestion involved in the numbers holding the opposite belief, or doing the other thing, is to be successfully resisted.

The second group consists of the conditions affecting the circumstances in which the suggestion comes. Suggestions which fit into the mental context, more particularly those which are in keeping with the mood of the moment, tend so far to be accepted. There are some people who naturally tend to react to a direct suggestion by saying or doing exactly the opposite of what is suggested. We call such people contrasuggestible, and under certain circumstances most people can become contrasuggestible. With such people the only way to get a suggestion accepted is by so moulding the mental context and background that, when a certain situation arises, or a certain idea comes into the mind in the ordinary course, the desired attitude towards it will be adopted. The power of this kind of suggestion depends on the fact that the course of action or belief we desire presents itself to the individual as his own. This is the secret of the useful and not uncommon art of getting people to take the course you wish in the belief that they are taking their own way and guiding their own action—the gentle art of managing people.

The third group consists of conditions affecting the mode in which the suggestion is given. The general principle here is that anything which gives the suggestion what we may call impressiveness tends to favour its operation. An assertion made confidently or authoritatively, or reiterated over and over again, tends by the way in which it presents itself in consciousness to inhibit opposing ideas. We tend to believe, for example, what we are constantly reading in leading articles, so that we often unconsciously adopt the politics of the newspaper we take in, though starting with politics of the opposite colour. This is also one of the secrets of successful advertising and successful salesmanship, and one of the reasons why advertisements take the forms they usually take, Gigantic lettering, a striking presentation. lighted letter, and figures appearing against the dark background of night, high up on the roof of some tall building, reiterated statements meeting the eye a hundred times a day—all these indicate the ways in which the advertiser applies this particular part of the psychology of suggestion.

The psychological status of the tendency we call suggestibility and the process of suggestion is by no means clear. There is evidently a close relation to the gregarious instinct and to the negative self tendency. The phenomena have also much in common with the phenomena of what has been called ' ideomotor action.' The theory of 'ideomotor action ' is that, apart from antagonistic influences, an idea of action tends to pass into the corresponding act. There is the psychological difficulty that an ' idea,' if this is taken to be purely cognitive, can have no power to produce action. But an ' idea,' in such a sense, never occurs in human experience. All our ' ideas ' are tinged with feeling or emotion, and bound up with incipient movements of various kinds, degrees of complexity, and degrees of prominence. In the concrete 'idea' there are affective and motor factors, and in these we must seek the explanation of ' ideomotor action.' So also of suggested ' ideas ' which become beliefs or lead to action. Hence the essential part of the process of suggestion would seem to be the elimination of antagonistic ' ideas.' More than this, however, is needed to account for some of the effects produced under abnormal conditions, as, for example, hypnosis. Whether the something more demands that we should recognize suggestibility as a definite instinctive tendency is another matter.[1]

[1] See for an excellent treatment of Suggestion, Baudouin: "Suggestion and Auto-suggestion."

CHAPTER VI

PLAY, RELAXATION AND MIRTH

PLAY is relaxation and recreation for the adult, but it is the serious business of the child. This seeming paradox expresses no more than the naked truth. The function of play in the life of the adult is to enable the organism, body and mind alike, to recover from the effects of strain due to strenuous labour involved in earning a living, or at least in satisfying the more or less exacting demands of the real world and modern civilized life. In the life of the child, on the other hand, the main function of play is to prepare him for the serious activities of adult life. As a leading authority has put it, the child does not play because he is young, but he is young in order that he may play. That is to say, the period of childhood and youth is essential in order that the human being may acquire those complex modes of behaviour, physical and mental, which are necessary to enable him to fill his place in the world, and it is largely through play that those complex modes of behaviour are acquired.

Psychologically play is differentiated from work or serious activity by two characteristics, and it is in virtue of these characteristics that play performs these functions for child and for adult. In the first place play is the outcome of an instinctive tendency to play, and hence the activity in play is felt as valuable for its own sake, and without reference to the results produced by the activity. In work, on the other hand, the value resides in the result produced, in an end outside the activity itself, and no matter to what extent work may become play, as we say, or yield pleasure in the performance, still the value is ultimately found in that which the work produces. At first sight it may seem as if the fact that in a game we seek to attain some end beyond the mere activity is inconsistent with the statement that in play the end is in the activity, but more careful consideration will show that even in a game a large part of the satisfaction is still in the activity, quite independently of the result, and in many cases the end is a more or less artificial end, invented, as it were, in order that we may play.   But of games we shall speak again later.

   In the second place there is a marked difference between the whole mental attitude and mental background in play and work respectively.   This difference is best described in terms of the contrast between belief and make-believe. In belief we are conscious of something real, existing independently of ourselves, to which our actions must adjust themselves, if we would attain our ends.   In work or serious activity this attitude of belief is present.   Our activity is with reference to a real, independent world ; the ends we seek belong to a system of real ends and real values, existing and subsisting independently of us, and recognized by others as well as ourselves.   In make-believe all this is reversed. The world of make-believe is a self-created world, and, while we may strive to adjust ourselves to the conditions of that world, we do so knowing all the time that, if we so choose, we may alter these conditions, that we are under no compulsion to act in accordance with them, or even to act at all, unless in so far as we place ourselves under compulsion. So with the ends we seek and the values we recognize.   These are only ends and values in the make-believe world we have created for ourselves, not in the real world which is independent of our whims, wishes, and desires.   In play the attitude is in the main precisely this make-believe attitude, characterized by freedom from the pressure of the conditions of an independent real world, by the ' don't have to ' feeling, and by the sense—it may be more or less vague—that the condi-

tions and ends are of our own choosing, and owe such validity
and value as they possess to our own volition.

This second difference between play and serious activity
obviously serves to place games distinctly with play in
opposition to work, even if the first difference fails. In playing
a game we detach ourselves from the world of real life, with
a detachment which is of the nature of dissociation. The
more absorbed we become in the game the more complete
is the dissociation. But, on the other hand, if in a game
real ends become dominant, so that the activity is pursued
not for its own sake, or for the attainment of the end of the
game as a game, but for the sake of those real ends which
belong to the system of real ends controlling our activity in
the real world, the game so far ceases to be a game, the play
becomes ' earnest.' The transition from play to earnest
is very common in the games of children, especially when
the self sentiment becomes active, and is not unknown in the
games of adults.

The function of play in the life of the adult is, as we have
already indicated, to give relaxation, to free temporarily
from the pressure of real life. This function it performs
because of the dissociation which characterizes it. The cares
and worries of the work-a-day life are laid aside, and the
complexes which belong to that life dissociated ; the inhibitions and repressions of the underlying, natural, elemental
man are at the same time removed, and the tension which
these inhibitions and repressions carry with them is effaced.
In order to understand why play gives relaxation and recreation, and so restores the tone of mind and body, soothing
the jangled nerves, infusing new vigour and strength into
the jaded spirit, it is necessary to remember that the conditions of modern civilized life impose an almost intol rable
strain and burden on the natural man. The civilized man
is an artificial product ; he is not yet completely evolved—
indeed far from completely—as a natural man. All major
conflicts may be resolved by repression or by sublimation,
but many minor conflicts are daily and hourly going on.
And even though major conflicts are resolved, this by no

means implies the entire quiescence of the primitive in man. Consequently the maintenance of civilized life must always involve a strain; the daily work, and the daily round of duties and obligations, many perhaps irksome, may often make that strain an acute tension. It is in virtue of the relief it affords by dissociation from this strain and tension that play exerts its recreative and recuperative influence in the life of the adult.

With respect to the child the position is slightly different. He, at least, is free from the strain and tension of the adult's life. He can be on the whole natural most of the time, though even in his case inhibitions and repressions begin early, and increase their range and scope with the passing years, so that even with the child—the child of school age more particularly—the recreative function of play cannot be wholly ignored. At the same time this is not the important function in the child's life, in which indeed play is far more prominent than such a function would explain or lead us to expect. The child's life is largely play; play is his serious business. This is so because play is necessary for his development. He plays himself into the activities, the interests, and the duties of the adult, in such a way that, when these activities, interests, and duties become serious, he is prepared to answer the call of the real world, and act efficiently in the real world.

This 'preparation theory' of play, as it is called, was developed in modern times by Karl Groos, but interesting anticipations of it are to be found in psychology as early as Malebranche. Briefly expressed, the theory is that play is a necessary stage in preparing the young of the higher animals and the human child for adult life, since at birth many of the instincts in the case of the higher animals, and more especially in the case of the human being, are not sufficiently developed or established to fulfil their functions, and this development and establishment takes place by means of play. It is a common observation that the modes of play vary according to the species of animal, and that the forms of play exhibited by any species resemble the characteristic forms of adult behaviour of the same species. The kitten, for example, springs on the piece of paper or the dry leaf as the adult cat springs on the bird or the mouse. The young kid or the young calf, on the contrary, will not spring on a piece of paper or a dry leaf, however much and however long it may be trailed in front of them, but they too have their forms of play, prophetic of their activities when fully grown. In accordance with the theory, therefore, we must suppose that instincts show themselves before they are actually required by the needs of life, and that they do so in order that they may be developed so as to meet those needs when they do arise. Hence the theory accounts not merely for the fact of play, from the biological point of view, but for the forms which play takes.

It is obvious that the function of play, on this view, is very closely related to the function of imitation, as already described. But, while play is essentially the means by which native modes of reaction, or those already partially acquired, are developed and established, imitation is essentially the means by which new modes of reaction are acquired. In actual development the two tendencies co-operate in the most intimate way, and are sometimes so closely interwoven that it requires some analytical power to separate the elements characteristic of each tendency in the total activity. The exercise and development of general processes and functions, sensory, motor, and intellectual, are due to both tendencies, operating independently or together. To a still greater extent do they co-operate in the exercise and development of special processes and functions, in the various groups of organized games, for example. In some games, as in games of combat or competition and hunting games, the part played by imitation is not particularly prominent; in other groups, like social, domestic, or family games, which are largely occupied with impersonations, imitation plays a very prominent part; in games of skill belonging to all groups, where the game itself requires a considerable amount of learning, imitation has an equally important part to play.

The relation of play to art and the enjoyment of art, to the

comic, to laughter and merriment generally, has been emphasized by many psychologists. Some psychologists have even
found in the play tendency the origins of art, and others have
based on it a psychological theory of laughter and the comic.
It seems worth while therefore to attempt to make the
relation clear between play and art, on the one hand, and
between play and laughter or mirth, on the other. A
complete theory of art or of laughter is out of the question
here. Even without such a complete theory, it ought not
to be impossible to accomplish the task we are undertaking.

It must be postulated that the play tendency is to be
regarded, not as a specific reactive tendency, because it is
not evoked by specific situations or kinds of situation, it is
not directed towards specific ends, it is not characterized by
any emotion of a specific quality, but as a general tendency
to be classed with imitation. Each and all of the specific
reactive tendencies, and more particularly the emotional
tendencies, may operate in the play way. The forms which
our play may take, the ends which appeal to us in our games,
are not determined by the play tendency itself, but by these
specific tendencies operating through play. For example, it
is not primarily because of the play tendency that we pursue
with zest a hunting game, but because of the hunting tendency ; it is not because of the play tendency that games of
combat and competition appeal to us, but because of the
fighting tendency, or the self tendency, or both. In other
words, our actual behaviour in play is what it is, and our
emotions are what they are, because our behaviour represents
the activity, and our emotions are the emotions, of specific
tendencies, which are operating, as we have said, in the play
way, not because that particular behaviour, and those
particular emotions, are characteristic of the play tendency.
Play may show itself in any form of behaviour, and it may
have as its accompaniment any one of the primary emotions.

Artistic creation seems to bear precisely the same relation
to the original tendencies and the primary feelings and
emotions. In artistic creation the activity is also, like the
play activity, exercised for its own sake. Undoubtedly then

artistic creation and the play activity must be regarded as very closely related to one another. From this point of view artistic creation might be considered as merely one direction which the play activity may take. But artistic creation and the appreciation of its results involve the æsthetic emotions. Do we in that fact find a differentia by means of which art can be marked off from play ? It would appear so. The æsthetic emotions are not different from other human emotions, but are æsthetic in virtue of the mode in which they are evoked, not in virtue of what they are in themselves. Nevertheless, in so far as artistic creation involves artistic appreciation and the æsthetic feelings and emotions, and in so far as the value of the activity lies in this element only, it must be regarded as different from the play activity, which does not necessarily involve the evoking of æsthetic feeling and emotion, and certainly does not aim at that. Artistic creation may be a development of the play activity, and from some points of view is perhaps rightly regarded as such, but is certainly not the play activity in its naïve form, and bears distinguishing marks which are not to be found in pure play.

Before leaving this point it may be well to define æsthetic feeling and emotion somewhat more closely. Emotion may be evoked directly through the presentation of the appropriate situation, through association, sympathetically, or by empathy. In the last case only do we have æsthetic emotion in any strict sense, though the term is often extended to cover certain instances of sympathetically induced emotions as well. The process called empathy is the process of feeling ourselves into an object or situation, so that we temporarily, as it were, become the object or situation, losing in the process our own identity, being literally absorbed in the object. " The trees of the field clap their hands, the little hills shout for joy, great mountains have a voice, break forth into singing, look abroad with silent brow ; there are souls in lonely places, the moanings of the homeless sea, the sullen river, and the woods waving and muttering." [1]

[1] Mitchell : " Structure and Growth of the Mind," p. 150.

When such words describe for us a real experience, such experience involves empathy, and this is the root and the stalk of the æsthetic emotions.

We are left with mirth and laughter. Several psychologists have asserted that man is the only animal that laughs. If that were so, it would be comparatively easy to distinguish laughter from play. But the only foundation for the statement appears to be that we do not among animals find those ' spasmodic contractions of the chest,' and those peculiar grimaces and sounds, which we identify with laughter in the human being. To argue therefrom that animals do not laugh is as sound as to argue that the lion must be a vegetarian because we find no knives and forks in his pantry. Psychologically mirth and laughter are much more than the spasmodic contractions, grimaces, and sounds. That the psychological phenomena are found among lower animals does not admit of a doubt to any one who has carefully watched a puppy, a lamb, or a young rabbit.

Theories of laughter are very numerous from Aristotle downwards. Most theories contain an element of truth, though nearly all are restricted in their application to a single phase or type of laughter. Thus Hobbes identifies laughter with the sudden development of a sense of our own superiority. "Sudden glory," he says, "is the passion which maketh those grimaces called laughter ; and is caused either by some sudden act of their own that pleaseth them, or by the apprehension of some deformed thing in another, by comparison whereof they suddenly applaud themselves. And it is incident most to them, that are conscious of the fewest abilities in themselves ; who are forced to keep themselves in their own favour by observing the imperfections of other men." Bergson holds that the specific character of the comic is a ' mechanical rigidity ' where you expect to find th adaptability and mobility of life, "the mechanical encrusted upon the living." Freud suggests that laughter is due to the partial freeing from repression of aggressive and sexual tendencies normally repressed into the unconscious. It could easily be shown that all three theories are true to the facts they are intended to cover, but hopelessly inadequate to cover all the facts.

The first principle that must underlie any theory of laughter is that laughter is an expression of joy. Joy, as we have seen in a previous chapter, is not an emotion, but the character of a whole group of emotions. In the joy emotions, one and all, an instinctive tendency is finding satisfaction so rapidly or so abundantly that action is unable to keep pace with feeling. Note the two conditions, rapidity or suddenness, and abundance or excess. As each may independently give rise to joy, so each may independently evoke laughter. But the laughter evoked by abundance is more characteristically the laughter of the child, the laughter evoked by suddenness the laughter of the adult, though neither is exclusively the characteristic either of one or the other. A second principle that must underlie all theories of laughter is that, as joy emotions may be evoked directly through association, sympathetically, or by empathy, so may laughter be evoked in all these ways, and all may co-operate in a single case—laughter at a humorous anecdote, for example, or a joke.

But we cannot develop a theory of laughter here. The point which we would particularly note is the effect of the sudden withdrawal of repression, the sudden disappearance of tension, in producing mirth and laughter. It is especially here that play and laughter come close together. Why do we laugh at the following :

An Irishman in a museum is gazing with interest at a copy of the "Winged Victory." "What may yez call that ?" he asks an attendant.

"That is a statue of Victory, sir," is the reply.

"Victory, is it," says Pat, surveying the armless and headless figure with greater interest than ever; "begorra, thin, I'd like to see the other fellow."

Or this :

The priest waited till Pat came out of the public-house and then accosted him with : "Pat, didn't you hear me calling ?"

"Yes, your reverence, I did," was the reply, "but I had only the price of one."

In the first case there is Pat's ignorance of art, and we may laugh out of our superiority of knowledge ; but surely this is not the real and fundamental occasion of our laughter. The second example seems to make evident the laughter-producing element of both. Pat insinuates—quite innocently, no doubt—that the priest ' wants a drink ' at his expense. The insinuation finds an echo in our more primitive self repressed by the customs and taboos of culture and civilization, and it is the sudden and temporary freeing of the primitive natural man that produces the laughter.   There can be no doubt that the same explanation holds in the first case.   What laughs in us is the primitive, elemental pugnacity, suddenly released, and triumphing over an imaginary adversary.

It would seem, then, that Freud has laid his finger on one main cause of mirth and laughter, though he has interpreted his facts much too narrowly and one-sidedly, while Hobbes with equal acumen and equal one-sidedness has seized upon another aspect of the central phenomenon. Release from restraint, removal of repression, free and unimpeded activity of the natural man, especially if occurring suddenly and unexpectedly, is a frequent cause of mirth and laughter.   But such free and unimpeded activity of the natural man and such removal of repression are also characteristic of play. Hence we should expect to find, as we do find, that play and mirth go hand in hand.   But while play naturally predisposes to mirth and laughter, it is not itself the source of mirth and laughter.   The source is the joy emotion of which laughter is the expression.

CHAPTER VII

DEFENCE MECHANISMS

IN the last chapter we discussed one aspect of our emotional experience—the joy aspect—in its relation to play and relaxation. We must now look for a short time at the other side of the picture. Our whole life of feeling is essentially bipolar, as we have seen. On the appetite level we have pleasure and unpleasure ; in the emotional accompaniments of the reactive tendencies we have joys and sorrows, and joys and sorrows at the higher levels where the appetites and primary emotions combine and interweave in the most complex fashion. No human life is exempt from pain and sorrow. In most human lives the pendulum swings continually between the two poles of feeling. A psychology of everyday life which neglects the many important phenomena of the sorrow pole cannot be regarded as anything but inadequate and incomplete. All these phenomena have deep human interest, many are of grave significance to the educator and the social worker, and not a few are of moment to the medical man.

Consider the fundamental facts once more. From childhood onwards the human being has to react to a real world over which he can exercise only a limited control, and has to adjust himself to conditions of this real world, by modes of behaviour showing all degrees of passivity and activity, submissiveness, constructiveness, active resistance. In the course of this reaction and adjustment he experiences pleasure and unpleasure, or joy and sorrow, both through direct contact with real things and real conditions without, and through the realization, or the reverse, of the ends of the impulses acting from within. It is the ineradicable characteristic of human nature to seek to maintain or return to the pleasure or joy, and avoid or flee from the pain or sorrow, but the necessities of adjustment may at any time forbid the one or the other. Hence there will be conflict between tendencies, which may be resolved, as we have seen, in successful repression or sublimation. But if the conflict is not resolved, what then ? There may be pains and sorrows which it is impossible to avoid, and yet we cannot help seeking to avoid ; there may be ends which we cannot attain, but which nevertheless we must inevitably continue to strive after ; there may be ' sorrow's crown of sorrow ' in the memories of the past. What are the psychological phenomena under these conditions ?

Let us begin with the reactions to pains and sorrows, which we cannot avoid, but which we cannot help seeking to avoid. The most common reaction of the human being to such conditions is by means of what has been called a ' defence mechanism.' We set up a defence against the disagreeableness, it may be consciously, but more often unconsciously, the effect of which is that the disagreeableness is either not allowed to enter our clear personal consciousness at all, or is compensated for in such a way as to give us an agreeable experience instead. The phenomena of the defence mechanism are exceedingly interesting, and will repay somewhat detailed consideration.

The simplest of all defence mechanisms is illustrated by the process we call self-sophistication. This process is not difficult to understand. We have, let us say, a strong desire to act in a certain way that is inconsistent with some principle of conduct we recognize. Self-sophistication consists in first of all convincing ourselves that it is not only right, but our positive duty to act in that way. We have now constructed a defence against the shame, regret, or remorse, which would otherwise be involved in our acting in a way inconsistent with the principles we profess and with our self-respect, and we can act as we desire with the agreeable sense of doing our duty, so securing the pleasure desired, and at the same time retaining our good opinion of ourselves. Thus, as a recent writer [1] has pointed out, we all recognized in theory the duty of economy and frugality in war time. Practically, in many cases, we kept on enjoying such luxuries as we were able to procure and afford. We frequented picture-house, concert, theatre, or golf-course, to preserve our mental or physical health. We could not let the confectioner, or the florist, or the milliner, or the bookseller starve, and so on.

But the most striking phenomena of the defence mechanism are exhibited in those cases where the disagreeableness, which is defended against, arises from some defect or inferiority in ourselves, real or imagined. It is a well-known biological and physiological fact that, where an organ is inferior or defective, there is always a tendency for the life forces to compensate for the defect, so as, on the one hand, to protect the defective organ against situations with which it is not competent to deal, and, on the other hand, to find some substitute to perform the function which ought to be performed by it. The same process is seen in conscious life. Every human being is an aspirant for the good opinion of other people as well as of himself. The feeling of inferiority is disagreeable, with a disagreeableness the intensity of which varies with different natures, but is almost always sufficiently high. Any defect, therefore, which will tend to bring on any one the ridicule, or condemnation, or bad opinion of others, or make him feel small or inferior in the presence of others, or anything painful or inferior in his own eyes, will be a motive for compensatory or defence measures, taken consciously or unconsciously. The result will be a defence mechanism of a simple or elaborate type, normal, or semi-pathological, or quite pathological, in its character.

Thus an individual, let us say, is a hopelessly incompetent workman in the line of activity he has chosen. In order to avoid confessing to himself his incompetence, which would involve the sense of inferiority as compared with others and

[1] Walter S. Hunter : " General Psychology," p. 64.

in the presence of others, he imagines that he is not being given fair play by his employers and his fellow-workmen. He is driven from one job to another, not by his own inefficiency, but by the persecution of his fellows—it may be even that the persecution is due to their jealousy because he is a better workman than themselves. The final outcome may be persistent delusions of persecution and the lunatic asylum.

The protective type of defence mechanism is still more frequent. In this case the individual tends to conceal the defect, or protect himself against situations which would reveal it, by poses, mannerisms, and the like. A deaf person may become so voluble a talker that his or her companions cannot get a word in. An artificial and stereotyped laughter or gaiety may mask real and painful self-consciousness and constraint in social intercourse. Camouflage, conscious or unconscious, is one of the most frequently encountered phenomena in all our social intercourse. The compensatory and substitutive type is almost equally common. A stammerer uses in his letters the longest words he can find, because he cannot use them in his speech. The blind may similarly revel in gorgeous description in visual terms, which their reading has made them familiar with, of scenes, dresses, and objects. This kind of defence mechanism is often of considerable social value, for the individual may develop those gifts and graces he has, so as to compensate, and sometimes more than compensate, for those which are defective.

Another common defence mechanism on the verge of the abnormal is forgetting. Disagreeable engagements, visits, commissions, experiences tend to drop out of our memory or to be dropped out, through repression and dissociation. According to Freud, the greater part, if not all, of our forgetting has a motive, and the most frequent motive is avoidance of the disagreeable. But repression is a two-edged weapon. What is repressed into the unconscious may not remain inactive, and will not remain inactive if it has a strong emotional colouring. The upper conscious life may be affected in all sorts of strange ways. Hence, again according to Freud, the causes of errors in speech or writing—*lapsus linguæ* and *lapsus calami*—are to be found in emotional complexes repressed into the unconscious.

Defence mechanisms are of great importance from the point of view of the care of children. They may make their appearance quite early, and with unwise treatment may exercise a ruinous influence on the whole after life of the child. The shapes which they may take are protean, and hardly any general principles can be laid down. We may, however, say that organ inferiority tends towards negativistic attitudes on the whole. That is, the child, conscious of his inferiority, avoids situations which would bring that inferiority into evidence by stubbornness, obstinacy, contrariness, unruliness of behaviour. Or it tends towards the establishing of weaknesses and defects, which seem to claim special consideration and prevent serious demands being made on him.

A practical point of great importance arises in connexion with the effects of punishment in such cases. If we assume that the aim of punishment is reform or improvement, we may say without hesitation that this aim can never be secured by such means. It is true there may be apparent success, but the apparent success will be due to the fact that we have merely driven the mischief deeper, sent it, as it were, underground, to reappear in other defence mechanisms and perhaps still more serious manifestations later. The whole theory of punishment requires to be revised in the light of recent work in this field. Punishment takes account only of the effects in the upper region of the personal consciousness. The effects in the deeper regions of the unconscious have hitherto been ignored. There are strong grounds for holding that these latter effects are nearly always bad, though of course not necessarily serious. When we are dealing with defence mechanisms, however, the whole position is altered. The defence mechanism is itself rooted in the unconscious. So long as the source remains unaltered, the child simply cannot help himself. Under these circumstances what possible good effects can we look for from punishment ? It

5

can obviously have but the one effect of intensifying the existing evil, of developing and complicating the defence mechanism.

Two cases may be cited which can be taken as summing up the whole situation. The first [1] is of a child, who exhibited neurotic tendencies very early, was considerably retarded in physical development, and more especially was outstripped by his brother. In the early period of life he found himself, or imagined himself, depreciated and belittled, and could not get into adjustment with the rest of the family owing to his feeling of inferiority. He craved to be equal to his brother, or any one who seemed to him strong and powerful, and this craving led to excessive covetousness, and to serious conflicts with his parents. The result was that he became a regularly unmanageable child at home, and in his school work also got farther and farther behind, and more and more out of harmony with his environment, until ultimately the path back to normality was closed against him.

In the other case [2] the subject as a child had suffered from a congenital digestive weakness, and consequently had to be denied many things which his father and brothers partook of freely and enjoyed. The result was, first of all, the development of envy and covetousness, and then of a tendency to take and store up for himself all kinds of sweet things. Gradually a more complex situation arose. The father, a hard, tyrannous man, dealt unwisely with his son's manifestations. As a result he became the object of a more or less unconscious hostility. Ambitious for his son's future, he placed great hopes in the promise of considerable oratorical ability which the boy displayed. Then the boy developed a habit of stammering, the initiation of which was due to a stammering tutor. The symptoms became more serious and firmly established. They were utilized in various ways by the boy, as, for example, to enable him to avoid the demands of his family in all kinds of things, to give him time to weigh his words before answering, and so on. The whole story is

[1] From Adler: "The Neurotic Constitution."
[2] From Pfister: "The Psychoanalytic Method."

too long to go into, but it was all of a piece, and the result a very serious deviation from normality in many directions.

We have still to consider the ' sorrows ' that arise from the failure to attain ends we must nevertheless continue to strive after. This is the standard condition under which the sorrow phase of the primary emotions and of all bipolar emotions is evoked. The sorrow will be poignant in proportion to the acuteness of the ' feeling tension ' existing, and that will be in proportion to the strength of the emotional tendency aroused, and the extent to which the satisfaction of the impulse is impeded or retarded. There are three possible states, as far as satisfaction of an impulse is concerned. The satisfaction may be immediate ; this will give us the joy phase of the emotion which has already been discussed. The satisfaction may be deferred ; this itself will tend to yield the sorrow phase. The satisfaction may be entirely denied, and all hope of attaining it utterly blasted ; this will give us the maximum of possible sorrow, as far as the particular impulse is concerned, which may find its natural outlet in tears and weeping, as the joy emotions under analogous circumstances find their outlet in laughter.

A state on the sorrow side somewhat analogous to play on the joy side, and related to tears in almost the same way as play is related to laughter, is the state we call worry. It will be recalled that the second differentiating characteristic of play activity was that the conditions, ends, and values, representing the real world, were dissociated. When we worry, on the other hand, we are unable to get away from the conditions of the real. We are obsessed with the things to be done, or that should have been done, and the pressure of the real is entirely unrelieved. There is nothing quite analogous to the other characteristic of play, but nevertheless the mental activity in worry, as in play, though in a different sense, leads nowhere. The ends are present with us, but in place of the practical attainment of the ends, there is ceaseless mental activity, planning and resolving, it may be, but passing continually from one subordinate end to another without any overt action to attain any one of them. If play is a relief from tension, and because of that a recreation, worry is a continuation of tension, without any relief through dissociation or through action.

Worry, as a relatively fixed state characterizing the mental life, is a long step in the direction of complete defeat. But while there is no confession of and submission to defeat, the tension and strain must still continue, and the defeat itself may ultimately involve that graver condition known as ' neurasthenia.' Neurasthenia is a pathological condition which cannot be discussed here. All that we need say is that it represents, on the one hand, this state of continual tension, on the other hand, numerous defence mechanisms, psychological and physiological, developed against the ' sorrows ' involved, and the final issue in an inability to make the necessary reactions and adjustments to the world of the real, with a mental state of which a highly emotional consciousness of this inability is the predominant characteristic.

CHAPTER VIII

PERCEIVING

HITHERTO we have been dealing almost entirely with that aspect of our experience which we may call the inner aspect, the forces and systems of forces that determine our behaviour from within. But our behaviour is behaviour with reference to a world that is without, and our experience, in another aspect, may be said to mirror the world that is without, in such a way, at all events, as to enable us to choose our time and manner of acting so as to fit these to external conditions. That aspect of our experience which renders this possible is called the cognitive or knowing aspect. It is the aspect we usually think of in connexion with experience, as it is the aspect upon which the attention of the older psychologists was almost wholly concentrated.

All our knowing is based originally on that direct and immediate apprehension of objects and situations, which we call perceiving. Such apprehension, if it is of external objects, depends on the present effect of the objects on our sense organs. What we see, hear, touch, smell, taste here and now, we perceive; what we heard or tasted an hour ago, yesterday or last week, we can no longer perceive, though we can still apprehend with the mind's ear or tongue, as it were. In the latter case we are said to image, or ideally represent, what we have formerly perceived. Without having perceived we could not ideally represent. Once we have perceived we may be able to ideally represent, when and as often as we please. Moreover in thinking—using the word in a strict sense—we consciously relate objects perceived or ideally represented, or aspects of such objects, or relations already apprehended. Hence the whole intellectual life is necessarily based upon, and rises out of, perceptual experience. Not only so, but, since intellectual activity is in general carried on in order that we may act more effectively, and in acting we are in direct and immediate contact with objects once more, the results of all intellectual activity return to modify and correct perceptual experience in manifold ways. Starting from perceiving the complete intellectual circle returns to perceiving again.

The two most important characteristics of perceptual experience are : (1) that it is always experience of one single object, and (2) that it is a present-moment consciousness, experience of the ' here and now.' Both these characteristics are fundamental. Together they indicate clearly the kind of consciousness we should have, were we confined to perceptual experience, and the kind of consciousness many of the lower animals must have. We should be conscious of a series of situations following one another, as so many separate wholes, bound together perhaps by some indefinite feeling of belonging together, if occurring in the working out of some instinctive tendency, but without our having any consciousness of the first when we were perceiving the second, or of the second when we were perceiving the third. There is on record an interesting pathological case which throws some light on the kind of consciousness the purely perceptual would be. That is the case of Voit, Grashey's patient.[1] Voit's consciousness was not purely perceptual, but ideal representation was much impaired. When asked the colour of snow, he could not tell, unless he saw snow. If it was winter time, and there was snow on the ground, he went to the window and looked out ; if it was summer time, he was quite unable to say, whether snow was black, white, green, or yellow. Asked how many legs a horse had, he watched the street till a horse passed, and then replied " four." On one occasion he was asked the colour of blood. For a moment he

---

[1] See Störring : " Mental Pathology and Normal Psychology."

was at a loss, then pressed out a drop of blood from a pustule on his hand, and answered "red."

The mental product of the process of perceiving is called a percept. We must not think of the percept of an object as simply an impression made on our minds by the object acting through the sense organs, and still less as a picture or image of the object on the brain. The actual experience is of the nature neither of a picture nor of a simple impression. In the case of the adult human being at all events it is much more complex than we are apt to think. Our experience of objects affecting our sense organs at the present moment is modified by our past experience of the same or similar objects, by the setting or context in which we perceive the objects, and by our own feelings and purposes at the moment. It is true that it is the impression on the sense organs that makes the experience what we call perceptual, and that forms, as it were, the core of the percept, but nevertheless there are numberless cases where the actual impression on the sense organs is of so little significance to us that we should be puzzled to state exactly what it is. We look out of the window and see that the streets are wet. What is it we actually *see* ? We hear a friend's voice at the door, or in the next room. What do we actually *hear* ? Half the difficulty of the beginner in learning to draw is due to the fact that he must represent what he actually sees, not the meaning of what he actually sees, and the meaning is what dominates his ordinary consciousness, while the sense impressions themselves may hardly be attended to at all. Independently of past experience and the mental setting, our feeling with regard to it, and our reaction upon it, have as much to do with making the perceptual experience what it is, as the impression on the sense organs, and in many instances a great deal more.

Though we do not usually recognize all these factors as playing a part in our perceiving, they have only to be mentioned for us to be able to identify them in many familiar cases. The whiteness of the sugar, which is at the present moment affecting us through the organ of vision, comes to us modified or qualified by a sweetness, which we do not see, but which nevertheless affects what we do see ; the whiteness of snow is similarly qualified by a coldness which we do not see, and yet it somehow seems that we do. The yellow of an orange drags into consciousness with it a fringe of weight sensations, sweet sensations, acid sensations, visual sensations even of the side away from us. From no direction, that we can regard a cubical box from, do the visual impressions give a cubical box, yet we see the cubical box notwithstanding. But these do not represent the only type of contributions from within to our experience of the object affecting us from without. Watch several people trying to find the hidden face in a puzzle picture, and you will be astonished, and not a little amused, to note how blind one person is to what another sees clearly, in spite of the fact that the sense stimulus from without is identical in every case. Familiar objects are perceived differently by different people according to their different interests. The sunset is perceived very differently by the artist and the sailor ; a mountain looks very different to the geologist, the lowland farmer, and the highland shepherd. The botanist and the naturalist see in a country walk what the ordinary pedestrian entirely overlooks, and the botanist may see what the naturalist does not see, and vice versa. The sailor sees the loom of the distant land, where the landsman sees nothing but a stretch of water to the horizon, and this, not because he has more acute vision, but because he knows what to look for, so that faint signs which are quite invisible to the landsman, stand out clear and distinct to him, as meaning something he is familiar with.

Even this is by no means the whole story. We tend to see and hear what we look for and expect to hear, it may be when the actual visual or auditory sense data afford scant justification for the experience they become to us. Equally is this the case under the influence of any strong emotion. The extent to which what we perceive depends on the mind that perceives is worthy of special note, in connexion more particularly with the psychology of deception. The clever conjurer, no matter how closely and suspiciously we watch him, can make us appear to see what we know with absolute certainty to be impossible. The conjurer's success is due to the fact that he either draws our attention to what is unimportant, and succeeds in doing the really significant things undetected, or makes us infer from certain things that certain other things have actually occurred, though they did not occur. In either case we fill in from within all that is necessary to make the whole experience what he intends. All the time he is, as it were, playing on the mind that perceives, and falsifying our experience in spite of the things that actually occur before our eyes. In so doing he merely utilizes, and perhaps intensifies the effect of, phenomena which are of everyday occurrence in our perceptual experience, and illustrates on a large scale the falsification to which the knowledge we obtain from direct perceiving is liable.

Such facts as these ought to be kept in mind in an examination of the evidence for various spiritistic manifestations. The medium has all the advantages of the conjurer, and he has the further advantage of dim light or darkness, of expectation, readiness to believe, often a highly emotional yearning and craving to believe, on the part of the witnesses. How unreliable the evidence can become, even of the trained and critical observer, with respect to what he has seen under much more favourable conditions, has been experimentally demonstrated over and over again. In the light of such demonstrations, the evidence of the great majority of the witnesses of spiritistic manifestations, however honest and sincere they may be, must be regarded as utterly worthless.

Other facts of our everyday life, of what we might call an opposite kind, illustrate in an equally interesting way the part which the subjective factor plays in perceiving. It not infrequently happens, when we are looking for something, that we fail to perceive it, even when it is, so to speak, 'under our very nose.' We may actually handle the object, laying it aside perhaps to look underneath it, and fail to perceive it as what we are looking for. At first sight this seems inconsistent with the principle that we see what we are looking for or expect to see. But the phenomena are more complex than they appear on the surface. Till recently the ordinarily

given explanation was ' absentmindedness.' ' Absentmindedness ' itself must have a cause, and Freud and his followers
put forward an explanation in terms of dissociation caused
by the ' unconscious.' This goes behind the mere general
attribute of ' absentmindedness ' in the attempt to explain
why we are ' absentminded ' in the particular case. This
explanation, which undoubtedly fits the facts in a great
number of cases, is that we fail to perceive because of an
unconscious wish not to perceive. We may desire to prove
that the object is not in a certain place, and ignore its presence
there. Or we may vaguely resent having to look for the
object at all, and so unconsciously determine not to perceive
it, feeling a satisfaction, not always unconscious, in our
failure.

The natural inference would seem to be, that, after all,
our knowledge of the world in which we live, if that in the
last resort depends wholly on perceptual experience, must be
exceedingly unreliable. The psychologist might well let this
pass for the truth without any undue qualms of conscience,
in view of the fact that it is less likely to do harm than the
opposite view, which is so generally held, that seeing is
believing, that what we ourselves see and hear must certainly
exist in the way we see and hear it to be. But the truth
ought not to be put quite in that way. Biologically the
function of knowledge is to guide our action, to determine
when, where, and how we must act, in order that our ends,
and the ends of life, may be most effectively realized. So
long as perceiving fulfils this function, it is fulfilling its true
function, and in order to fulfil this function perceptual
experience must not reflect the external world as it is in
the abstract for nobody in particular, so much as the external
world as it is in the concrete for us here and now, the external
world as it is in relation to our knowledge, our habits, and
our interests. This is precisely what perceptual experience
does, and on the whole adequately. To do so it must depend
upon inner factors, as well as on the nature of external things.
In a sense the very efficiency of our perceiving involves the
very errors and defects to which it is liable.

It is clear also that we *learn* to perceive, and this is part of what we call training in observation. The animal, or the new-born child can hardly be said to perceive at all, in the sense in which we perceive. The perceived world of the baby is as James put it, " one big, blooming, buzzing Confusion." Experience is simply a blurred, massive whole, and this blurred massive whole is for the baby the universe. There is no distinction between the Me and the Not-Me, still less between the experience and that of which it is the experience. In this great blur elements and parts become differentiated by the child's own reactions, guided by instinctive interests and impulses. Adjustment to ' this ' and to ' that ' separates the ' this ' and the ' that ' from the as yet undifferentiated whole. Movements of the body and limbs, and the experience of these movements, define still more clearly the ' this ' and the ' that,' and their relation to one another. The Not-Me is separated from the Me in so far as certain elements in experience are beyond control and demand adjustment and motor adaptation, while other elements, including the experiences of adjustment and adaptation, are under control. And so the process goes on, adjustments, and adaptations, and movements bringing definiteness and order into the child's universe. The process is indeed the same from first to last. Discriminating and perceiving are acquired through reacting, though the reacting may become more and more complex, more and more intellectual, and more and more subtle, as the higher mental processes begin to play their part.

The way in which we come to perceive space affords an admirable illustration of the kind of process that goes on in all its complexity. Our developed perception of space is the result in the main of the co-operation of touch, sight, and sensations of movement. Touch sensations and visual sensations have a vague ' spread-out ' character, which forms the basis of our perception of size and superficial area. Sensations on the skin, from the retina, and in the joints have also a character, which has been called ' local sign ' in virtue of which the sensation derived from one part is different from the sensation derived from another part. By means of our experience of the direction and extent of movement, points characterized by different local signs are defined in relation to one another within the vague ' spreadoutness,' which with the development of this position, direction, and distance within it becomes definite extension for us. Our perception of the third dimension in space is mainly due to vision, though in a rudimentary way it can be developed independently of vision. The accommodation of the eyes for near or more remote objects, the slight differences between the images of the two eyes, movements of the eyes, all yield sensations which serve as a cue for the perception of the third dimension. The larger and more complex visual world is thus ordered and arranged mainly through sensations of movement, on the basis of differences in local sign, in precisely the same way as the more circumscribed world of touch. It should, perhaps, be noted that relatively great distances from us are judged on the basis of other factors, such as apparent size, number of intervening objects, atmospheric effects, and the like.

The major part of the activities characteristic of our daily lives are carried on at the perceptual level. We act immediately on what we perceive, and the result of one act is the stimulus to the next, without our ever requiring to think of what we are going to do, or how to do it. In many cases the activity is impaired as soon as we begin to think about it, as in going down steps, for example. If a situation has to be dealt with immediately, we cannot afford to think how we ought to deal with it, but must act at once, and can only act on the basis of our perceptual experience. In all learning which involves the acquiring of skill or dexterity the perceptual level is in the same way supreme. In learning to play golf or cricket, whatever help a coach may give us, he cannot give us the necessary skill by describing what ought to be done. One thing only can give us the skill, and that is practice in doing what ought to be done. The reason is, of course, that a mere description may enable us to realize every step in the process imaginatively, but practice in acting will alone teach us when and how to act on the cues given in our sense experience. Our perceptual learning must proceed mainly by the method of 'trial and error,' as it is called. This is the predominant kind of learning, among the lower animals also, because perceiving plays the predominant part in their experience. In this method each individual act in a series of acts is selected and established by the fact that it succeeds in attaining the end aimed at, while the wrong acts and the unnecessary acts are gradually eliminated by the fact of their failure. The more complex the behaviour to be learned the longer it will take, and the time will increase much more rapidly than the complexity. This is the point at which the help of a teacher or coach becomes valuable. For the expert can prevent the tyro from many mistakes, which would be eliminated with difficulty later, if at all, and keep him along right lines at points where success and failure are too remote to exercise any determining influence.

Much experimental work has been done on perception since psychology first began to make use of experiment. Within recent years the practical application of some of the results of such work, both in education, and in the various branches of industrial and commercial life, has developed enormously. In education it is important to know the range of perception —the so-called ' span of apprehension '—at different ages, that is the number of objects that can be grasped in one act of perceiving ; it is important to know also the nature of the child's observation at different stages, the extent to which, and conditions under which, this observation may be falsified owing to the operation of different factors, the differences in the rate at which perceiving and reacting may take place, and so on. Many of the tests devised originally for educational purposes have been modified and adapted as tests of an individual's fitness for various occupations, and even as tests of the efficiency of workers at different times and under different conditions.

The earliest practical application of this kind was probably the employment of the ' æsthesiometric index,' as it is called, as an indication and test for fatigue. The æsthesiometric index is the distance apart two points—say of compasses—must be before they can be discriminated as two, when touching the skin simultaneously. This distance is also called the spatial threshold, and it varies enormously from one part of the body to another, being very small on the lips or the tips of the fingers, and very large in the middle of the back.   It has been found to vary also for the same place with the condition of the subject, and one of the conditions causing increase is fatigue.   Hence its employment as a test for fatigue.   It has now been shown, however, that it is a very rough and exceedingly unreliable test, if it can be called a test at all, owing to the great variety of conditions by which the spatial threshold may be affected.

Attempts have also been made to test fatigue by some test of the efficiency of perception.   A typical test of this kind, with wide possibilities of variation and of practical application, is the cancellation test.   The subject is asked to pick out and mark a certain letter or letters—or it may be a certain digit—in a page of letters specially arranged for the purpose of the test, or chosen from any suitable book or newspaper. A definite period of time is given, and the efficiency of perception is measured by the number of letters covered, the number of letters rightly marked, and the number of letters omitted or erroneously marked, all combined in a single 'efficiency coefficient.'

The experimental study of observation has also yielded important results, already alluded to, bearing upon the value of testimony, and the conditions under which, and manner in which, it may be falsified.   In particular it has been shown that the testimony of children, as we should expect, is very unreliable, and very easily falsified, the more so the younger the child.   Of course there are individual differences, but this is true even of the most reliable.   One very interesting difference between one child and another—and the difference also exists between adults—is very well brought out by a description test employed by Binet.   If different individuals are asked to write a description of some familiar object placed before them, it will usually be found that, while some of them describe the object as it really is or seems to be, or draw inferences from what they see in a way that would gladden the heart of Sherlock Holmes, others read into the object their own feelings about it, or wander off from the object before them to tell all they know about such objects in general. An illustration will probably make the difference clear better than pages of description. The object is a cigarette.[1] Here is the first type—the objective observer :

"A long, white, round object, composed of a paper cylinder filled with what is probably oriental tobacco. It is a badly rolled, uneven cigarette, and has been handled since it was pasted. In two places, to the right and left of the middle, the paper shows streaks, as if it had been twisted. Other horizontal depressions indicate that there has been some pressure exerted upon the cigarette, etc."

Here are two examples of the second or subjective type, one emotional, the other matter of fact.

"It is a cigarette. It is thin, long, somewhat wrinkled. Its shape suggests a kind of elegant ease. Is it the cigarette itself, or the memories that it awakes, that remind me somehow of a scape-grace ? The cigarette there, all by itself on the table, makes me think of the bad student that goes off in the corner by himself to smoke, etc."

"We have before us here a cigarette. Let us see how it is made. In the first place, the exterior envelope is of light paper, called silk paper. Then inside is the tobacco. Tobacco is a product that grows almost everywhere in warm or temperate climates. The leaves of this shrub are gathered, etc."

The most interesting experiments of all are those on the span of apprehension. In these experiments a number of objects must be exposed for a brief moment of time, sufficiently long merely for a single glance. Under such conditions it has been found that there is a definite and easily reached limit to the number of individual and unconnected objects that can be perceived at once. If, however, the objects fall into natural and familiar groupings, the individual may apprehend nearly as many groups as separate objects. Thus, if an individual can apprehend six separate and unconnected letters, exposed for a brief instant, he may be able to apprehend as many as five or six familiar words, and still more if they form a sentence.

[1] From Whipple : "Manual of Mental and Physical Tests."

By these and similar experiments great light has been thrown on the processes involved in reading. It has been shown that we do not perceive individual letters when reading ordinary matter, but word wholes. It has also been shown that we do not read by moving the eye continuously along a line, but by a series of rapid glances. We may have three or four such glances at each line. The movements in between are so rapid that it would be quite impossible for us to read while the eye was moving. We may have no consciousness of these processes in our own reading, but can easily watch them in another.

CHAPTER IX

SOUNDS AND COLOURS

FROM our sense experience of vision and hearing we derive most of the higher pleasures of sense, the æsthetic pleasures strictly so called, though much of the pleasure we derive from these sense experiences can hardly lay claim to the designation ' æsthetic,' but, on the contrary, as we shall see, is quite of a piece with the sense pleasures of taste, smell, and organic sensibility. Vision and hearing are entitled to be called the higher senses on other grounds, and from quite a different point of view. From them we derive the greater part, and the most clearly discriminated part, of our knowledge of the world in which we live. This is due, on the one hand, to the fact that both senses give us knowledge of what is distant, as contrasted with what is in actual contact with the body, and, on the other hand, to the fact that the elements and parts in the total sense experience at any time can be distinguished and separated much more easily in the case of these senses, and particularly vision, than in the case of the other senses, and more particularly taste, smell, and organic sensibility. Moreover, the feeling element —agreeableness or disagreeableness—is generally so pronounced in the experiences of the lower senses that the knowledge element is more or less masked.

" The whole gamut of the world's sounds," as Watt says, " falls into two halves, which are perfectly obvious in their extremes, although there is no clear division between them."[1] These two halves are musical sounds and noises. All the

[1] " The Psychology of Sound," p. 15.

6

sounds we hear in the crowded city or in the open country are a combination in varying proportions of these two. Physically sound consists of waves or vibrations in the air, and we hear sounds because these waves strike against the drum of the ear and are thence conducted to the sensitive endings of the auditory nerve.   In the case of musical sounds the waves follow one another at regular intervals—they are periodic; in the case of noises there is an irregular mixture and succession of shocks.   Most sounds belonging to both categories are more or less complex.   Few noises, that is to say, are without a trace of some sort of tonal element, and few musical sounds without some slight admixture of noise.

When there is a single smooth succession of regular waves falling upon the drum of the ear we experience what is called a pure tone.   An approximately pure tone can be produced when appropriate measures are adopted, but the musical sounds with which we ordinarily have to deal are by no means pure tones, and the music lover would not desire that they should be.   If, for example, we strike one of the keys of a piano the result is a musical note, but not a pure tone.   The note is in fact composed of a number of different tones sounding together, one of which—the fundamental—is more prominent than the others and gives the pitch of the note. Such a complex musical sound is called a ' clang.'   The tones which compose it, in addition to the fundamental, are known as ' overtones,' many of them being easily distinguishable by a practised ear.   A simple and pure noise probably does not exist.   At any rate the great majority of noises give the impression of complexity.   By producing a number of musical notes simultaneously we can obtain practically all gradations between a musical sound and a mere complex noise ; we cannot, however, obtain anything but noise by producing a number of noises simultaneously, though we can often get a musical note by producing the same noise over and over again with sufficient frequency, as in holding a card against a rapidly rotating toothed wheel.

Pure tones differ from one another in loudness, volume, and pitch, clangs in these characteristics, and also in relative complexity and in the relative prominence of the tones composing them. As we have already indicated the sounds given by musical instruments are clangs, consisting of a fundamental tone and its overtones. The relative prominence of certain overtones is one of the chief means by which we distinguish the sound of one musical instrument from that of another. It is also largely by means of the relative prominence of certain overtones that we distinguish one human voice from another, either in speaking or in singing. Overtones are produced by vibrating strings, or columns of air, because not only is there vibration of the string or air column as a whole, but there is also vibration of the half, the third, the fourth, and so on. Thus, if we produce from a stretched wire, the fundamental tone corresponding to 200 vibrations per second, we may also find the wire giving tones corresponding to 400, 600, 800, etc., these latter being the overtones.

The sounds given by the human voice in speaking are very complex, and are partly tonal and partly of the nature of noises. These sounds can be artificially produced on the gramophone, but with additions which give a certain character to the reproduction, by means of which it is always possible to distinguish it from the human voice. This difference in character in the gramophone reproduction is also due partly to changes in the emphasis on certain overtones, and to the addition of certain noise elements, both due to the nature of the vibrating substances and the conditions under which they are vibrating, and hence analogous to the differences between one human voice and another.

The tone series, so far as it is audible to the human being, extends from a note of about 16 vibrations per second to one of 30,000 to 40,000. Notes below the lower limit are felt as a series of separate puffs or shocks, those above the higher limit, if we are conscious of them at all, as a mere hiss without any tonal element. The ordinary musical scale represents but a small part of the total range of audible tones, a grand piano yielding notes between 26 and 4,000, and the organ between 20 and 8,000. There are curious differences between individuals as regards audible range. The case is on record of an American who was unable to hear the singing of birds, and who took all the statements about it in literature for poetical phantasy like the statements about the music of the spheres. As a rule the hearing of elderly people is somewhat contracted at the upper end. Thus in the South of England there is a saying that no one over forty ever hears a bat squeak. Ability to distinguish difference of tone—pitch discrimination—is exceedingly acute for the middle portion of the ordinary musical scale, a difference of half a vibration per second or less being distinguishable with practised observers. Towards the upper or lower limit discrimination becomes much less acute, and near the upper limit a difference of some thousands may not be noticed.

Pure tones by themselves are relatively characterless, though individuals may show a certain amount of preference for high or for low tones, as the case may be. Pure tones are, however, exceedingly rare, and difficult to produce. What we ordinarily produce from almost any source of musical sound, are clangs. With clangs, even when sounded alone and without any musical context, there are marked feeling reactions, and marked individual differences as regards preference. The phenomena are analogous to those of colour preference, and will be considered more fully under that head.

When two different notes are sounded simultaneously new and interesting phenomena make their appearance. In the first place, other notes are heard in addition to the fundamentals and their overtones. Such additional notes may or may not have any existence in the external air. They are known as 'combination tones.' One combination tone is the 'summation tone,' a tone with a vibration rate equal to the sum of the vibration rates of the two fundamentals. Other combination tones are 'difference tones,' with vibration rates equal to the difference between the vibration rates of the two fundamentals, or of one of the fundamentals and the overtones of the other, or of two overtones present in the complex. Thus, if two tones of 800 and 400 vibrations respectively are simultaneously sounded, we may hear in the complex the summation tone of 700, the first difference tone of 100, a second difference tone of 200, and possibly other difference tones between the overtones as well. These facts afford some explanation of the vast variety of effects possible in music.

In the second place, the complex sound produced gives an experience of consonance or harmony, on the one hand, and dissonance or discord, on the other, and when consonant gives rise to a peculiar and characteristic agreeableness, when dissonant to an equally characteristic disagreeableness. The physical and physiological basis of our experience of consonance and dissonance has given rise to some controversy. The view most commonly held is that consonance is due to the relative absence of ' beats ' in the complex, dissonance to the prominence of ' beats.' When two tones differing slightly from one another in vibration rate are sounded simultaneously, there is a rising and falling in the intensity of the sound, owing to the fact that the two series of waves interfere with one another, at some points tending to cancel one another, at other points to be added together. Such rising and falling in intensity we call ' beats,' and the number of ' beats ' always corresponds to the difference in the vibration rates of the two tones. Now in the complex produced by sounding together two notes rich in overtones, there is nearly always some beating, either between the fundamentals, or between the overtones, or between fundamentals or overtones and combination tones, but the beating may be merely enough to give a piquancy to the total experience, in which case we shall have the agreeableness of consonance in spite of the beating, and enhanced by it ; or, on the other hand, the beating may be prominent, harsh, and very unpleasant, when we shall have marked dissonance or discord. There are objections to this explanation of consonance and dissonance, into which we cannot enter here, but in the meantime, for lack of an alternative, it may be fairly said to hold the field, though Dr. Watt[1] has recently suggested a theory

[1] " Psychology of Sound," and " Foundations of Music."

which has much to commend it, and which would bring our pleasure derived from music into line with the pleasure we derive from form and colour.

Vision is the richest of all the sense departments, in the number and variety of experiences it yields, as well as in the value of these experiences for our knowledge and appreciation of the world in which we live. Our visual experience is dependent upon the waves of light which impinge on the retina of the eye. Waves of light are vibrations of the ether, and, as in the case of sound, there are definite vibration rates, between which alone the vibrations are experienced as light. These limits are represented by the two ends—red and violet—of the solar spectrum. The human eye is not affected by rays beyond either the red end or the violet end of the spectrum, though means can be taken to show that there are such rays, those beyond the red end being characterized by their heat-producing effect, and those beyond the violet end by their chemical action on sensitive substances. Light of a definite colour is normally produced by light waves of a single wave length, white light by a mixture of waves of different wave lengths in certain proportions, a mixture either of all the colours of the spectrum, or of the three colours red, blue, and green, or of two colours suitably chosen.

So important is the sense of sight that few indeed of the phenomena of vision might not claim mention in a psychology of everyday life. If a preference must be shown, that preference is due to some of the main phenomena of colour. Of these, the mutual interaction of the colours we call complementary, colour blindness, colour preferences, and the feeling effects of colour generally have a manifold significance and importance for our daily lives. On these phenomena we shall therefore concentrate our attention.

Two colours are mixed by the rapid rotation of a disc composed of sectors of the respective colours. Any two colours may be mixed in this way and in any proportions, the results produced varying with the colours selected. If, for example, we mix red and yellow in this way, we can get all hues intermediate between the two, from a slightly yellow-ish red through orange to a slightly reddish yellow. If, however, we mix our red instead with a certain shade of green, a different kind of result is obtained. We can never get a reddish green or a greenish red, but, as we add more and more green to the red, the disc will continue to show a red becoming less and less saturated, that is with less and less red in it, until we get a grey without any trace of either red or green. Beyond this the disc will show a green, at first faint, but increasing in saturation, until we get a saturated green. In this case, therefore, the colours do not mix to produce an intermediate hue, but cancel one another, and at a certain point, when the two colours are present in certain proportions, we have, as has been said, a colourless disc. Such pairs of colours are called complementary. For every colour a com-plementary colour can be found. The mixing of pigments may not produce the same result. The mixing of red and green pigments will produce a yellow if the particles of both pigments, as is usually the case, reflect yellow light as well as red or green. The red and green cancel one another as before, but the yellow is left.

Complementary colours are also contrast colours. A patch of red on an otherwise colourless surface, tends to give the rest of the surface a greenish hue, provided the edges of the red are not too strongly marked. The best effect is obtained by covering the whole with tissue paper. When the edges, either of a coloured spot on a colourless background, or of a colourless spot on a coloured background, are too well-marked, the contrast effect is subjectively destroyed. Red and green side by side tend to intensify one another because of this contrast effect. The same is true of blue and yellow, or of any colour and its complementary.

Moreover, if we look at a patch of colour for a short time—say 20 seconds—and then turn our eyes on a colourless surface, white, grey or black, we see on that surface a patch of the complementary colour, which may appear and fade away a number of times. The same effect may be obtained by simply closing the eyes after we have looked at the coloured spot. If the whole visual field is coloured, say by wearing green glasses, we gradually cease to be aware of the colour, but, on removing the glasses, find the whole field coloured red. An interesting illustration of the same effect is often obtained in a railway carriage, if the sun is shining brightly on one side. When the train goes into a tunnel we see a bright patch of green to the side at which the lighted window was. The explanation is that the light from the side window, before affecting the retina, is coloured red by passing through the network of blood-vessels in the coating of the eye. Consequently when the light is withdrawn the complementary colour develops.

It is obvious, therefore, that colour effects, like tonal effects, may come to be somewhat complex. To some extent we ignore changes in colour due to association with other colours, either simultaneous or successive. Objects come to have for us a definite colour, and we persist in seeing that colour, even when the conditions are such that our sense experience is really of another colour, or when we cannot help being conscious of the real colour it is greatly weakened by the fact that the object has for us an absolute colour. For example, the light of a red sunset falling upon snow gives a red tint to the snow, but we are so accustomed to see snow as white, that, unless we try to match the colour we see, it seems to us far less red than it is in actuality.

Colour blindness [1] is the name by which we designate failure to distinguish certain colours or all colours. Some forms of colour blindness, or at least of colour defect, are much more common than is generally supposed, and unless special tests are employed the individuals may be totally unaware throughout their lives that their experience of colour is in any way different from other people's. There are three main types of colour blindness. The most frequent is marked by inability to distinguish unsaturated red and greens from one another, and from certain greys and browns. This type is rare among women, but occurs in one out of every twenty

[1] The condition of colour blind persons is best described by saying that their colour series, from red, through yellow, green, and blue, to violet, and back, through purple, to red, has in it two gaps, of varying width, which appear uncoloured or grey.

or thirty men. Seeing that we employ red and green on an extensive scale for signalling purposes, this defect is obviously of great practical importance. A very rare type of colour blindness is marked by inability to distinguish blues and yellows from one another and from certain greys. The third type is total colour blindness, in which all colours appear as different shades of grey. All of us are totally colour blind as far as the margin of the retina is concerned, hence in indirect vision, and the vision must be more direct to enable us to see red and greens, than for blues and yellows. It is impossible for the engine-driver to tell whether a signal seen in indirect vision is red or green, whereas he might, with the same amount of indirectness, distinguish blue and yellow. The facts of colour blindness and allied facts seem, therefore, to indicate the desirability of substituting blue and yellow for red and green in signalling, and a suitable arrangement of white lights would be best of all.

The most interesting section of the psychology of colour vision is probably that dealing with our colour preferences, and generally the feeling values and effects of colours, singly and in combination. Much experimental work has been done in this field in recent years, and with results that would seem to have an important bearing on many things with which we are in daily contact in ordinary life, on pictures, on schemes of decoration and furnishing, on dress, and the like. It has been argued that the different feeling effects of different colours are due to associations rising from our own experience. But investigation has clearly shown that, while such associations may explain the feeling effects and colour preferences in some instances, they do not explain the greater part, and the more typical part, of the effects. For instance, it has been proved that infants of three or four months old show definite colour preferences,[1] and one would hardly assert that in such cases associations with previous experiences were at work.

One investigator[2] found that individuals could be arranged in classes, according to the point of view from which they

---

[1] Valentine : " Experimental Psychology of Beauty."
[2] E. Bullough. See articles in " British Journal of Psych.," Vols. II and III.

regarded colours, and expressed preference for one colour rather than another. In the experiments the subject was asked to say whether he disliked or liked each of a number of colours exposed under precisely the same conditions, and the reason for the like or dislike, so far as the subject could give a reason. On the basis of the reasons given the subjects fell into four classes :

1. Those who liked or disliked a colour because of its objective qualities, such as purity, saturation, dullness, and the like. (This would seem to be a secondary rather than a primary feeling effect, an effect due to a judgment or estimation of the colours with reference to some criterion.)

2. Those who liked or disliked a colour because of its direct effect on them, sometimes a physiological effect, as soothing, warming, dazzling, and so on. (This is a primary feeling effect, which seems to be quite analogous to the feeling effect of tastes, smells, etc. There is a case on record of a man who had been blind from birth, and who had had his sight restored by an operation, feeling sick at the sight of yellow.)

3. Those who liked or disliked a colour because of its associations, because it reminded them of experiences pleasant or unpleasant. (This is another secondary rather than primary feeling effect.)

4. Those who liked or disliked a colour because of the feeling or character they read into it, as jovial, sympathetic, aggressive, etc. (This is the æsthetic effect *par excellence*.)

Of thirty-five subjects only three belonged definitely to the fourth class. When combinations of colours were employed, however, the æsthetic judgment became much more frequent. The same four classes were distinguished by Valentine in experiments with musical intervals.[1]

When we investigate the feeling effects of combinations of colours, and particularly when we are dealing with complex objects like pictures involving forms as well as colours, two principles emerge in terms of which we are able to interpret a large proportion of our results. These are the ' principle of balance ' and the ' principle of facilitated attention.' The

[1] Valentine: " Experimental Psychology of Beauty."

former is probably the more purely æsthetic. In any complex arrangement of colours or forms, certain colours or forms or parts of the whole appear to have ' weight,' and the apparent weights may determine the agreeableness, or the reverse, of the arrangement of the forms or colours relatively to one another. Weight may be objectively conditioned, depending, say, on the hue, brightness, or saturation of the colours themselves. Some colours or shades are ' heavy,' as it were in their own right. In schemes of decoration, as in the wall-paper of a room, the effect will in general be displeasing if heavy colours are placed above ' light ' colours, because there will be a disagreeable feeling of top-heaviness or pressure. Weight may also be subjectively conditioned by our interest, and this is especially true of pictures. The balance of a picture is not determined solely by the colour scheme, but largely also by our interest in the various parts and objects depicted.

As we have said, the principle of balance is equally applicable to forms and colours ; the principle of facilitation of attention is applicable mainly to forms. Whenever our attention or mental activity is facilitated we have an agreeable experience, and a disagreeable experience whenever it is checked or baffled. Anything which suddenly ceases to be what it apparently set out to be produces such a check, and is experienced as disagreeable. But the check may be only temporary, and may enhance the total pleasure when we discover that our first impression was only partial, and that there is a larger whole, or an aspect of the whole, which we did not at first perceive. This indicates one possible explanation of the fact that it needs training to appreciate the best art or the best music. The untrained simply cannot see the larger wholes, and consequently their mental activity is constantly being checked or baffled without the more than compensating pleasure being experienced.

But it is applicable to much more homely matters also. Why is the effect usually disagreeable when we have a picture framed, showing a large white space of the mount ? Apparently because this large, white, unfilled space causes this baffling of the attention.   It pretends to be part of the picture because it is in the frame, and it therefore draws the attention to it, just as the background, and generally the accessories of the picture, draw the attention.   But these have something to give the attention, some contribution to the effect of the whole.   In certain circumstances the white of the mount might also have the same kind of effect, and then it would not be felt as disagreeable, but in general it only draws the attention to baffle and disappoint it.   The same principle is applicable to the pairing of pictures.   If we experience a mental jerk in passing from the one picture to the other the effect is disagreeable.   It is no less disagreeable if the attention is checked by the opposite characteristic, the too great similarity of the pictures.

It is interesting to note how far advertising posters satisfy æsthetic conditions.   We generally find two conflicting tendencies manifested in them.   On the one hand, there is the tendency to give as great prominence as possible to the object advertised.   This must be regarded as the essential thing in the advertisement as such.   On the other hand, there is the tendency, subject to the condition that the attention be attracted, to make the colour schemes and the whole arrangement moderately agreeable.   Where the two tendencies conflict the first ought in general to have the preference. This is not always done.   For example, a familiar advertisement of ' Oxo ' would probably be improved as an advertisement by making the ground greenish-blue in place of blue, or by making the lettering bright yellow in place of red, but æsthetically the present colours are perhaps preferable.   So long as nothing strongly disagreeable appears in a poster, the main principles guiding the colour scheme should be those arising from the interaction of colours with one another. Yellow lettering on a blue background with a yellow border will make a stronger visual appeal, than if we substituted red for yellow or green for blue.

As regards colour preference it has been shown that there are marked differences between child and adult, between savage and civilized, and less marked, but still distinct, differences between men and women, between different social classes, and, if results obtained in the George Combe Psychological Laboratory in Edinburgh are reliable, between Orientals and Occidentals. With young children red seems to be the favourite colour, but gradually drops down the scale of preference as the child grows older, blue taking its place at the top, and earlier with girls than boys. Adult men arrange the colours in order of preference—as far as educated Englishmen are concerned—in some such way as this : green, blue, red, white, yellow, black ; adult women put them in this order : blue, green, white, red, yellow, black. As we have indicated, however, interesting differences appear with difference in social status, in nationality, in education, and there are individual differences as well.

CHAPTER X

TASTES AND FLAVOURS

"TASTE, smell, as well as hunger, thirst, nausea, and other so-called common sensations, need not be touched on in this book, as almost nothing of psychological interest is known concerning them." So writes William James in his "Textbook of Psychology," and such a statement seems to indicate that we have a very unpromising topic for the present chapter. Nevertheless, we shall perhaps find more of psychological and popular interest in this apparently very unpromising field, than James' statement would lead us to expect.

The term 'taste' is popularly used to describe sense experiences which are generally complex, and often not tastes at all. When we are told that we cannot by taste alone distinguish a piece of apple from a piece of onion, we are apt at first to be a little incredulous. The incredulity lasts till the moment in which we put the statement to the test of actual experience. If we stop our nostrils with cotton-wool, so as to prevent as far as possible any air currents through the nose, which would involve smell, and then have placed on the tongue in succession a small piece of apple and a small piece of onion, astonishment takes the place of incredulity, when we realize that it is quite impossible to say which is which.

At the same time our ordinary language points to some complexity in our taste experiences which we recognize, for we use another word 'flavour' to describe something which may be included under taste, but which nevertheless differs in some way from taste proper, though we may be quite unable to say what the difference is. The difference is that flavour is largely smell. We cannot, however, say simply that taste is taste, and flavour is taste plus smell, or at any rate we must not think in saying so that we have cleared up the whole difficulty. Analysis shows a much greater complexity than is represented by the two words taste and flavour in our ordinary speech. As popularly used, taste—excluding flavour—still covers not merely taste sensations proper, but also touch sensations, temperature sensations, and organic sensations. Flavour may involve all these, and smell in addition.

We may begin by considering the phenomena of taste. The organs of taste are found mainly on the tongue and soft palate, and are more widely distributed in the child than in the adult. They consist of the so-called taste buds which lie in clusters in the small projections known as the fungiform and the circumvallate papillæ. Only by the stimulation of these taste buds can sensations of taste be produced. The whole interior of the mouth yields touch and temperature sensations, and the pharynx and alimentary canal organic sensations. Hence the liability to confuse these sensations with the sensations of taste. If a small pinch of powdered marble or any similar substance be placed on the tip of the tongue, we get touch and temperature sensations in the same way as if the powder were placed on any other part of the skin. If a pinch of sugar be substituted for the powdered marble, we get touch and temperature sensations as before, but in addition the taste sensation we call sweet, and this kind of sensation is to be got only by stimulation of the taste buds. Even on the tongue itself there are areas which yield no taste sensation, because there are regions of the tongue in which no taste buds are to be found. One such region is the middle of the tongue. If a portion of the middle of the tongue be partly dried, and the pinch of sugar placed on it, we get merely the touch and temperature sensations from the sugar as from the powdered marble.

By careful experiment of the same kind we can also quite easily show that the different taste sensations given by the taste buds are four, and no more than four—sweet, bitter, salt, and sour.   Some of the papillæ yield only one of these tastes, others two, or three, or all four.   In all such experiments it is necessary to cut off the interference of smell by plugging the nostrils, and also to dry the tongue to a certain extent, so that only the spot intended may be stimulated.   All substances which have a taste are soluble.   If the tongue be not dried, so far as to prevent the solution of the substance spreading, other parts than the parts intended will be stimulated.   On the other hand, if the tongue be completely dried, there will be no liquid to dissolve the substance, and it will not even stimulate that spot.

Seeing that we have suggested the method in which experiments on taste must be conducted, this seems a good opportunity to describe these methods in fuller detail, in order to illustrate the kind of work that is done in the psychological laboratory in the study of our sense experience. Let it be said that the main aim in psychological experiments is, on the one hand, to isolate the different factors so as to study each independently, and, on the other hand, to control the conditions as far as possible, so that the effect of each change of conditions may be clearly traceable. This is one of the main reasons why we employ apparatus, and sometimes very complex and delicate apparatus, in psychological work.   If we can secure our aims without apparatus so much the better.   But in any case our experimental work will be successful in the exact measure in which we are able to isolate the various factors in the processes we are studying, and control the conditions.

The materials and apparatus necessary are : a magnifying glass—a concave mirror if we use ourselves as subjects—a set of fine camel's hair brushes trimmed even at the point, pipettes, a carafe of distilled water, cotton wool, the various solutions to work with, and several glass vessels for various purposes.

Subject and experimenter seat themselves at opposite

sides of a table. The subject extends the tongue, flattening it over the lower lip as much as possible. The experimenter, using the lens to get a magnified image, makes a rough map of it, marking the contour and median lines, and putting in characteristic and easily recognizable groups of papillæ. Some of the more prominent of these papillæ are localized very carefully on the map and numbered; these are the papillæ with which the experimenter is going to work. The subject, after this is finished, with nostrils plugged, and eyes closed, takes up as comfortable a position as possible, and waits for the stimulus. The experimenter takes a brush out of the glass of water in which it is standing, dries it with cotton-wool, and dips it two or three times in the solution to be used. At the word " Now," the subject dries the tongue by squeezing it against the roof of the mouth, and then extends it; the experimenter sets the brush down gently and evenly on the selected papilla, taking care that the solution does not run, and holds it in place for two or three seconds, or until the subject recognizes the taste and withdraws the tongue. The subject then describes his experience and the experimenter records the description. Finally the subject washes out the mouth thoroughly with water, and one experiment is finished.

Some of the facts obtained from such experimental work have already been mentioned. Of the others the facts of taste contrast and compensation are probably the most interesting. We have already described colour contrast, both simultaneous and successive, as well as the phenomena of colour mixing. Quite analogous phenomena occur in the case of taste, though they are neither so easily nor so clearly observed.

If, using pipettes, a drop of a fairly strong salt solution be placed on one side of the tongue, and simultaneously, on the other side, a drop of distilled water, the distilled water will often be tasted sweet. Individuals vary a great deal with respect to taste, and the contrast effect may not be obtained under these conditions. If this is so, we may substitute for the distilled water a very weak solution of sugar,

7

which under normal conditions is not tasted as sweet. This will almost always become quite definitely sweet, when the drop of salt solution is placed on the tongue simultaneously.

Successive contrast may also be obtained, but not so easily. In this case strong solutions must be used. The mouth is first filled with the salt solution, then rinsed, and filled with distilled water or the very weak sugar solution. It has been found that bitter is the only taste that cannot be produced by way of contrast. Both salt and sour produce sweet, though sour may sometimes produce salt as its contrast effect, and sweet may produce either salt or sour.

We have seen that certain colours neutralize one another and produce a colourless sensation. In the case of taste we have an analogous phenomenon, and this time it is a rather familiar one. A moderately weak salt solution may be neutralized by the addition of a sugar solution, so as to become practically tasteless. On the other hand, if we use a strong salt solution, the result of neutralizing it is not a tasteless solution, but a solution that gives a new taste, generally called alkaline, which was at one time supposed to be a simple primary taste.

What was called a metallic taste was similarly at one time considered a simple taste. It has now been shown to be complex, and it may at least be imitated by certain mixtures of salt and sour. The main difficulty in imitating complex tastes is in producing the necessary touch, temperature, smell, or organic accompaniments of the taste. The analysis of a complex taste is much easier than its synthesis. Thus the ' taste ' of lemonade may be analysed into a sweet taste, a sour or acid taste, a smell—that of lemon—a temperature sensation, and a slight pricking or pain sensation. So the ' taste ' of lime-water is made up of a weak sweet taste, an organic sensation of nausea, a sensation of temperature, and a biting sensation of combined touch and pain; the taste of tea of a bitter taste, a smell, a temperature sensation, and an astringent sensation. But it is quite a different matter to produce the complex ' tastes ' of lemonade, lime-water, or tea, by combining the known elements which compose them.

We may make the transition to smell by considering some complex 'tastes,' which, so far as their characteristic qualities are concerned, should rather be called smells—which are therefore flavours rather than tastes. Wine tasters and tea tasters should be called wine smellers and tea smellers, for it is the smell, not the taste, that yields the necessary information. It is easy to see how smells are so much involved in tastes. There are connexions behind between the cavity of the mouth and that of the nose, so that if there is any current of air through the nose, while an odorous substance is in the mouth, the smell forms an almost inseparable part of the total experience. That is why we cut off all such air currents when we are investigating taste sensations.

If a series of eight taste solutions be prepared, two of each kind, such as honey and New Orleans molasses for sweet, strong coffee and tea—not quite so strong as to be astringent —for bitter, lemon juice and dilute cider vinegar for sour, and clam bouillon and beef bouillon for salt, the significance of smell in determining flavour can easily be shown. First take the solutions in any order, close the eyes, and let a spoonful of each be placed in the mouth, allowing both taste and smell to operate by leaving the nostrils open, and thoroughly rinsing out the mouth between each spoonful. No difficulty will be found in identifying the solutions. Next take them in pairs, the two sweets, the two bitters, and so on, close the eyes, plug the nostrils, and avoid breathing out while the liquid is in the mouth. The identification of the tastes will now be found a much more difficult matter.

So close is the connexion between taste and smell that we often characterize smells by words that really describe the associated tastes. Thus the air in a room where toffee is being made smells 'sweet.' Obviously it is the associated taste that is sweet. The strength of this associative connexion can be demonstrated by another simple experiment. Ask a subject to smell first a piece of baker's chocolate, and then some tincture of peppermint. In all likelihood he

will describe both as smelling ' sweet.'   Now let the subject
taste them, and he will experience, and probably manifest, a
shock of surprise at the taste of the second, so strong is the
association of the smell with a certain taste.

In contrast to the comparative poverty of taste in different
qualities, smell is exceedingly rich, so rich that it has not
yet been found possible even to classify the different smells
in a satisfactory manner.   All that has been found possible
is to group smells in nine classes : such as ethereal smells, as
the smell of fruit ; aromatic smells, like that of camphor ;
fragrant smells, like the odours of flowers ; ambrosiac smells,
like the smell of musk ; and so on.   The elementary smell
qualities it has hitherto been found impossible to determine.
Smell is also vastly more sensitive than taste, and in its
sensitivity even in the human being we have an interesting
sidelight on the important part which it plays in the lives
of many of the lower animals.   In the case of some of the
animals smell should probably be reckoned as one of the
higher senses, in the same category with the sense of sight
and the sense of hearing.

Like taste, though not perhaps to quite the same extent,
smell is complicated by other sensations.   It sounds somewhat paradoxical to say that a substance like ammonia has
comparatively little smell.   The statement may be read in a
standard psychological textbook that it is odourless.   The
characteristic pungent sensations obtained by smelling
ammonia are chiefly cutaneous sensations and organic
sensations depending on its irritating action.

By means of an apparatus known as the olfactometer we
can measure the acuteness of smell in different individuals,
and the sensitivity of the organ of smell with respect to different odours.   Great individual differences are revealed in
such experiments.   It is not at all rare for an individual to be
entirely unable to perceive certain odours.   Many people,
for example, are unable to smell prussic acid.   Cases are
on record of individuals, whose smell was otherwise normal,
but who were unable to smell one or other of substances
like benzoin, vanilla, mignonette, violets, etc.   At the other

extreme there is a case cited by Scripture [1] of a " woman in charge of a boarding-school who always sorted the boys' linen after the wash, by the odours alone." In smell experiments, as in taste experiments, precautions must be taken if the results are to be of any value. Every care must be taken to keep the air of the room free from any odour. The breathing must be slow and even ; sniffing increases the dilution with air, and therefore diminishes the intensity of the smell. The organ of smell must also be in its normal condition.

The most interesting of the phenomena of smell, and from many points of view the most important, are the phenomena of exhaustion or fatigue. These can be demonstrated very simply and very effectively. Take two flowers—roses, say —with a fairly strong perfume. The roses should be of the same kind, and as nearly as possible of the same size. Make certain by a preliminary sniff of each that they do have a strong perfume. Now smell one, by preference the smaller if there is any difference in size, for a minute, and then smell the other. It will be found that the second has little, if any, smell.

Experimenters have taken advantage of the fact that smell is easily fatigued to analyse smells, and the classification of smells is partly based upon this kind of experimental work. It has been found, for example, that if smell is exhausted by camphor, other odorous substances divide themselves into three groups. One group will give no smell, a second group will show no change, a third group will still give a smell, but a different smell from their normal smell. We can only explain these facts by assuming that in the organ of smell some cells or fibres respond to one smell, some to another. The smell of camphor fatigues one set of cells or fibres, and no substance which stimulates the same set can then be smelt, while substances which stimulate other sets are smelt as usual. Substances which are not smelt after exhaustion with camphor are therefore classed in the same group with camphor. Further, the change of smell in the third group

[1] " Thinking, Feeling, Doing," p. 96.

indicates that these smells are complex, that one element belongs to the same group with camphor, and that the new smell is the smell of the other element or elements.

If we smell nitrobenzene continuously we get in succession three different odours: first, for a short time, the smell of heliotrope, then that of bitter almonds, and finally that of benzene.   Hence the smell of nitrobenzene must be a complex consisting of at least three simple smells.   In almost all alcoholic solutions or tinctures the original odour disappears after smelling for a short time, to be replaced by the odour of the alcohol.   For this reason overflavoured vanilla ice-cream is said to taste of whiskey.   Hence not only do such phenomena give us a means of classifying the different smell qualities, but they also seem to offer us a method of analysing complex odours.

The phenomena of contrast and of compensation are not so easy to study in smell as in taste.   There is considerable doubt whether contrast phenomena occur at all.   As to compensation it is more or less recognized in everyday life that odours may neutralize one another, and this is one reason for the use of perfumes.   But the phenomena are by no means easy to study experimentally, because the phenomena of rivalry, as it is called, often appear in smell and considerably complicate matters.   If we smell at one and the same time two different odours, any one of three effects may be produced.   We may get a complex odour produced by their combination.   Or they may neutralize one another.   Or we may get one odour alternating with the other and sometimes also with the combined odour, in rivalry.

It is very significant that, whenever we wish to carry out experiments on feeling in the psychological laboratory, we almost invariably employ tastes or smells as stimuli.   We do so because taste and smell are very strongly marked by their agreeableness or disagreeableness, and a comparatively primitive and simple type of agreeableness and disagreeableness, not the complex æsthetic type.   This is one reason why taste and smell are of relatively small value for definite and clear knowledge.   It is also the reason why common acquired appetites are developed in connexion with these senses, and more particularly taste.

The most important result of the high feeling value of taste and smell has already been indicated in Chapter IV, when we were describing Cannon's findings with respect to the physiological effects of feeling and emotion. Good cooking is an aid to digestion, not merely because it makes food more digestible, but indirectly by making it appetizing and agreeable. If the food and the general accompaniments of the meal are such as to produce a pleasant or agreeable experience, the general physiological results of such an experience tend towards good digestion, and where the opposite is the case the opposite effects are produced.

CHAPTER XI

REMEMBERING AND FORGETTING

BY means of memory our past is made available for present use. "As a merely perceiving self," says an American psychologist,[1] "I am bound to this desk, this room, this plot of ground ; but as a remembering self I live through once more the exhilarating adventures and the beautiful scenes of my past experience, and as a creatively imagining self I am hampered neither by now nor by then." Through memory our past becomes an instrument by means of which we think, will, and act in the present, and, but for remembering, we could only think, will, and act, if we could do any of them, on the basis of the experience of every present moment.

In strictness the words 'memory' and 'remembering' should not be employed as if they were practically synonymous terms. Memory is a character of all organic life ; remembering is a matter of personal consciousness. In the present chapter, while presupposing the fact of memory, we shall have occasion to speak often of remembering, and its correlative forgetting, but seldom of memory itself. Remembering means the reinstatement of past experience as idea in our present consciousness. What cannot be so reinstated, temporarily or permanently, we are said to forget. Forgetting is a failure to remember, not a failure of memory.

We are so preoccupied with the importance of remembering

---

[1] Calkins : "First Book of Psychology."

that we usually fail to realize that forgetting is of almost equal importance. Without forgetting our remembering would be of little value to us. If the past persisted in reproducing itself in full detail we should never get forward, but must continually keep reproducing the past over and over again. This condition is to a certain extent manifested in the phenomenon known as "total recall." Most of us know people who give every detail of any event they may be relating, irrelevant and essential following one another without distinction, and in wearisome monotony. Some novelists are very fond of introducing this kind of character, and if we have never met such a person in real life, we are certainly familiar with him or her in fiction. Miss Bates in Jane Austen's "Emma" is an illustration, as James has already pointed out.

"But where could you hear it ?" cried Mrs. Bates. "Where could you possibly hear it, Mr. Knightley ? For it is not five minutes since I received Mrs. Cole's note—no, it cannot be more than five—or at most ten—for I had got my bonnet and spencer on, just ready to come out—I was only gone down to speak to Patty again about the pork— Jane was standing in the passage—were not you, Jane ?—for my mother was so afraid that we had not any salting-pan large enough. So I said I would go down and see, and Jane said, ' Shall I go down instead ? for I think you have a little cold, and Patty has been washing the kitchen.' ' Oh, my dear,' said I—well, and just then came the note."

Remembering of this kind not only makes an individual wearisome to other people, but it makes him ineffective both in thought and in action, because remembering cannot perform its function unless it is in some sort selective, unless it gives us the past with some kind of perspective. On the other hand it is well to remember that the ability to recall details when they are wanted is of undoubted advantage. James points out that probably no one was ever "successful on a voluminous scale," without possessing this ability in a high degree, and that what he calls the folio and quarto editions of mankind, like Luther, Leibniz, Sir Walter Scott, have all had it. So long as we keep in view the fact that the main function of remembering is to enable us to bring the past to bear on the actions and problems of the present and of the future, we have a criterion which will enable us to estimate the value of any kind of remembering and forgetting.

Neither remembering nor forgetting must be regarded as absolute. What we remember at one time we may forget at another time, and what we forget at one time we may remember at another time. It is said that a drowning man recalls all his past life in detail. Literally that is of course an impossibility, but the important truth the statement contains is that details of our lives, which have apparently been quite forgotten, may in certain circumstances reassert themselves in our experience, and more especially so under abnormal conditions. There is a case cited in textbooks of psychology of a man who, in an acute illness in hospital, began to repeat long passages in some language utterly unknown and unintelligible to nurses and doctors. Scholars were called in and pronounced the language to be Hebrew. The explanation—if it is any explanation—of the phenomenon was that many years before the man had been in the service of a distinguished Hebrew scholar, a professor in one of the universities, who was accustomed to read Hebrew aloud. Probably under normal conditions the man could not have repeated three consecutive words in Hebrew, and yet, years afterwards, he repeated long passages in delirium, at least in such a way as to enable scholars to recognize the language.

Remembering depends upon two fundamental characteristics of mental process to which we have already referred, conservation or retention, and cohesion or association. While both factors co-operate in all remembering, any individual instance of recall may be due mainly to association with what was previously in mind, or with what is in mind at the moment, or it may come into mind, as it were spontaneously. Spontaneous recall is not arbitrary or accidental. Freud is undoubtedly right in his contention that there is nothing arbitrary or accidental in the mental life.[1] Spontaneous recall is the outcome of processes going on below

[1] See " Psychopathology of Everyday Life."

the level of personal consciousness.   Conserved experiences are not stored up somewhere in an inactive condition, in a condition of hibernation, so to speak. It must be remembered that they represent modifications of a living system, and partake therefore in its life activity.   One kind of spontaneous recall, which is matter of familiar experience, has been designated 'perseveration.' It is exemplified by the tendency of an experience we have just had to repeat itself.   The process, temporarily submerged below the threshold of personal consciousness, as it were, rises above the threshold once more without the operation of associative factors. Associative factors may, however, operate below the threshold of personal consciousness, in which case we shall have the phenomenon of apparently spontaneous, non-associative recall, though in reality the recall is as much determined by association as those where the associations are obvious.

The conditions which favour conservation, and also perseveration, are clearly those conditions which cause an experience to impress itself deeply upon our minds.   They are summed up under what are usually, though quite erroneously, called the Secondary Laws of Association—primacy, recency, frequency, and vividness.   First impressions are proverbially lasting.   That is the law of primacy, and, subject to fairly obvious qualifications, it generally holds.   We remember better an event that occurred this morning, than an event that occurred a year ago.   That is the law of recency which plays a great part in the process we call cramming for an examination.   The more frequently a thing has happened to us the better we remember it.   That is the law of frequency, which underlies the method of repetition in learning. In all these cases the most important qualification we must add, in stating the laws, is 'other things being equal.' Lastly, whatever makes a deep impression on us at the time will tend to be remembered afterwards.   That is the law of vividness, and it is the most important of the four.

In virtue of cohesion or association, part of an experience always tends to reinstate the whole and the other parts. An admirable illustration of the simple operation of associa-

tion is given by James.   A father wishes to show off before
some friends the progress his rather dull child is making at
school.   Holding his knife upright on the table, he says,
" What do you call that, my boy ? "   " I calls it a knife,"
is the immediate and confident reply, from which the child
refuses to budge.   The father suddenly remembers that a
pencil, not a knife, is used in school, and taking a pencil
from his pocket holds it up in the same way.   The question
" What do you call that ? " now brings at once the desired
answer :   " I calls it vertical."   The knife did not reinstate
the desired piece of knowledge, because it had no association
with it, the pencil did, because it entered into the original
experience.

What are the main conditions on the association side which
will lead to the remembering of anything we wish to remember ?   First of all the closeness of connexion between the
thing we wish to remember and something we habitually or
very frequently have in mind.   This closeness may be the
result either of real connexion between the two things, so
that the one necessarily implies or involves the other, or of
their having been frequently associated together, or merely of
their being associated together under conditions which tend
to make the connexion an effective one.   Hence the more
we bring 'connexions to clear consciousness, the stronger
will be the associative bond.   It should be noted that association has apparent direction.   The connexion operates with
much greater certainty and facility in a certain direction—
the direction in which it has been laid down—than in the
opposite direction.   We can easily verify this by attempting
to repeat the alphabet or a familiar piece of poetry backwards
In the second place the more associations anything we wish
to remember has entered into, the more likely are we to
remember it.   Hence the more we know of any branch of
knowledge, the more easily we can remember facts connected
with that branch.   Hence also the more our knowledge is
systematized, the more facts are connected up with one
another to form a whole, the less likely are we to forget any
part.

Another phenomenon which plays a prominent part in all remembering and all forgetting, and also in all learning, both the acquiring of skill and learning by heart, is the phenomenon of interference. The best way to bring home to ourselves this phenomenon is by trying a simple experiment. Arrange five simple figures—five points will suit, full stop, comma, semicolon, colon, dash—repeated a number of times in a different order, in a number of lines, say ten, taking care that each figure occurs the same number of times in each line. One line might go like this :

.;, — : , — .; .;:, — ,:—.; —;,.:

If we now attempt to name the points as rapidly as we can, we shall get a curious result.   There is apparently no reason why we should not keep a constant time for each line, or perhaps show a little improvement as we get used to the task.   But as a rule we actually find considerable differences between the times taken for the different lines, amounting to as much as thirty or forty per cent. and these differences irregularly distributed.   For example, the times for the ten lines might read somewhat as follows (in fifths of a second) : 85, 80, 28, 40, 45, 82, 25, 40, 86, 42.   What is the explanation of this ?   Careful self-observation will probably reveal the checks now and then, when we want to say ' colon ' and ' comma ' or ' dash ' seems to thrust itself forward, often so strongly that it is actually spoken, or makes the word spoken a meaningless condensation.   We usually find, in such cases, that the name just spoken, that immediately preceding the check, was followed by a comma or a dash the last time it occurred.   As a result there is interference on the part of the association then formed, and such interferences are the chief causes of the variations in time for the different lines.

Interference operates in many very interesting ways. Thus a wrong impression, or a wrong association in learning will impede remembering in exact proportion to the extent to which it perseveres.   If the wrong impression is the first impression, or the last impression, if it is frequent, or if it is vivid, it may be a very serious obstacle indeed to accurate and easy recall.   It is easy to draw practical deductions. For this reason it is very important that the first impression should be clear, definite, and accurate, and time spent in securing this will be time saved in the long run. Further, in learning by heart of any kind, a hesitating and blundering attempt at recall may do positive harm. If we are brought to a standstill in attempting to recall, we should not guess, but apply to the book at once.

But by far the most interesting cases of its operation are those cases where the interference is due to some factor below the threshold of personal consciousness, or in the 'unconscious,' to use the ordinary phraseology. A submerged idea-complex, especially a repressed complex, may affect the stream of personal consciousness in manifold ways, some of which may be of the nature of simple interference of the kind described, delay, distortion, or temporary inhibition of certain ideas or words, while others are of a more radical nature, involving the absolute blocking of association paths —'dissociation' is the technical term—not merely for a short time, but for a long period, and even permanently. The new psychoanalytic psychology is full of illustrations showing all the different degrees. Jung's 'association method' is in fact largely based on interference phenomena. This method is an attempt to bring to light emotional complexes by asking the subject to reply to each of a series of familiar words with the first word that comes to mind, and then, after the whole series of words has been worked through, going over it again and asking for a reproduction of the reaction words given the first time. The time taken to give the response is noted in each case. Interference caused by emotional complexes may show itself in the undue lengthening of this time for particular responses, where the stimulus words have, as it were, touched the complexes, and often for several of the succeeding words also, in the failure of response or of reproduction, in unusual and peculiar responses, and so on. This method has met with a considerable amount of success in the diagnosing of mental disorders, due to emotional complexes, repressed or partially repressed. Attempts, which have aroused a good deal of public interest, have also been made to apply the method to the detection of crime.

Freud's psychoanalysis is a more elaborate and more radical method of procedure, based also on free association to a large extent, but relying on other lines of investigation as well, and more particularly on the study of dreams. We cannot go into a detailed description here. It is sufficient to say that for Freud, as for Jung, interference phenomena are important symptoms of the activity of complexes in the 'unconscious.' As we have already indicated, slight slips of tongue or pen, slight mistakes in carrying out intended actions, the unexpected forgetting of something that ought to be familiar, mislaying of objects, and a host of other small errors of various kinds, which are of daily occurrence in the lives of most of us, are regarded by Freud from this point of view, that is as symptomatic of interference directly or indirectly on the part of submerged complexes. That he is right in regarding them from this point of view seems undoubted. Whether the submerged complexes are always of the kind he suggests is another matter.

We have mentioned forgetting among interference phenomena. It must not be supposed that all forgetting is due to inhibition or dissociation. Subject to the qualification already made, that remembering and forgetting are relative, not absolute, we may say that there is gradual oblivescence, as distinct from dissociation, with respect to much of our experience. Casual and indifferent occurrences may, it is true, be conserved, but they are conserved as what they are, casual and indifferent, and that means they are forgotten in the ordinary sense. As causes of forgetfulness we have these three, *selection* and *interference*, which operate partly through inhibition and dissociation, and *oblivescence*, the result of lapse of time.

We must now consider briefly, from the point of view of learning, some of the practical results that follow from the known facts in the psychology of remembering and forgetting. Among the general conditions tending to efficiency of learning the first and most important is interest. We learn and remember most easily what we are interested in. The explanation of this in terms of what we know of remembering is not difficult. It is clear that our interest gives certain impressions an advantage over others, and they become for us more vivid. Further, in proportion to our interest, we are inclined to dwell upon certain things and certain thoughts, which involves frequency of repetition. Further still, anything that appeals to any of our interests finds numerous connexions with the other objects which appeal to the same interests, and these connexions are strong in proportion to the intensity of our interest. There is an interesting law, called by James ' Hodgson's Law,' in accordance with which certain elements in an experience are selected out and dwelt upon at the time—our principle of selection—because of our interest in them. Consequently being held before the mind while the rest of the experience fades, they have a further opportunity of forming associations with other objects, and generally with other elements in other experiences, in which we are similarly interested.

The operation of Hodgson's Law is often strikingly exemplified when we think on any scene or any occurrence in the somewhat distant past. This practically reduces itself, so far as we can recall it, to the points in which we were specially interested, and many falsifications of memory may be the result. The writer was on one occasion travelling in the same compartment ,with two elderly men, who had been close friends in boyhood and youth, but who had not met for thirty years. They were recalling some of their youthful experiences and escapades, and in one instance with rather amusing results. One asked the other if he remembered a certain occasion, on which they had both visited a certain house, and he described the various things that had happened. The other could not recall these things, but remembered another occasion on which they had both visited the same house, when various other things had happened. The comparing of dates and other circumstances were sufficient to convince a third person that both were speaking of the same event but obviously not to convince either of the persons more immediately concerned, for each to the end held to his opinion that "that must have been another time."

Hodgson's Law carries a valuable lesson for teacher, preacher, or lecturer. Most of us have had experience of the not infrequent result of a copiously illustrated speech, sermon, or lecture, when the illustrations are recalled readily and fully, but the main points have vanished. The obvious moral is that an illustration should never be employed for its own sake, because it is an interesting illustration or a good story, but only to illustrate some leading point, and that it should be of such a kind as inevitably to suggest the point which it illustrates.

A second important condition affecting the efficiency of learning is the formation of rational bonds of connexion. It is evident that rational associations economize effort of remembrance. The more the details fit together into a rational whole, the less need is there to remember them as details. All that we require to remember is the whole, or the principle which holds them together.

A third general condition which affects learning and remembering is the physical and mental state at the time when we are attempting to learn. Probably no commonly occurring state is so inimical to learning as fatigue. Many of the psychological tests for fatigue, in fact, are memory tests. It is certain that if we try to memorize anything, when we are either in physical pain or tired, we are practising very bad mental economy, and, unless there is some very special reason for our attempting to learn, even under such adverse conditions, we would be much better employed in playing whist, taking a walk, or going to the theatre, even from the point of view of progress in our learning.

In the technique of learning itself, there are two points which recent psychological experiment has shown to be of very considerable importance, the distribution of learning periods—important both in learning by heart, and in the acquiring of skill or dexterity—and the method of committing to memory anything we wish to learn by heart. We may consider them in turn.

8

If we have two hours to devote to learning—either the acquiring of skill or learning by heart—we can get a better result by devoting half an hour to the work on four successive days, than by working straight on for the two hours. The poorest result would be attained by working for two hours on end, a better result by working for an hour on two successive days, a still better result by working for half an hour on four successive days, and probably the best result of all by working for a quarter of an hour on eight successive days, or forenoon and afternoon on four. The same truth may be expressed in terms of repetitions. Assuming we are to give twelve repetitions to the learning of anything, our best distribution of these repetitions will be one a day for twelve days, and the worst twelve in succession on one day. The bearing of this on the value of short intensive courses is worth noting. The limits of the application of the principle are fixed by the time it takes for us to get adjusted and warmed up to our work. If our periods are too short, the working may never have reached its maximum of efficiency by the time the end of the period is reached, because we have not had time to warm up to our work.

If we have to learn by heart a piece of continuous poetry or prose, there are several methods we may adopt. We may read through the piece from beginning to end, over and over again, until we can repeat the whole, or we may divide it up into short sections and learn each separately. What are the respective values of these two methods? Miss Lottie Steffens, an American investigator, published in 1900 the results of some experiments which she had carried out with a view to answering this question. She found that both for nonsense syllables and for poetry the entire method gave the better results, not merely for permanent remembering, but also for rapidity of learning. This result has since been confirmed by a number of investigators, working with different kinds of material, and with different lengths of units, and it may be held as an established truth, that the entire method is more economical than the sectional method, so long as the material to be learned is homogeneous, for units up to 240 lines of poetry as far as the adult is concerned. Two American investigators, employing units from 5 to 240 lines, found that the longer the unit the greater the saving.

Both these important practical truths, which seem so contrary to what we should expect and to our ordinary methods of working, may be explained, at least partially, in terms of what we know of interference. By distributing our learning periods widely we allow wrong associations which have been formed time to fade away. The more recent an association is, or the weaker it is, the more is it affected by lapse of time. In general, if our learning is careful, the more recent and the weaker associations are the wrong associations. By allowing these to fade away, we avoid the possibility of their impeding our learning by interference. As for the sectional method of learning, it is evident that in using that method we are establishing unnecessary and false associations between the end of each section and the beginning of the same section, whereas the right associations are between the end of each section and the beginning of the next. Hence the lengthened time in learning by the sectional method is due to the overcoming of interfering associations. It is obvious also that these wrong associations are older than the right associations afterwards formed, and therefore with lapse of time the right associations may be the ones to disappear and the wrong to remain. Hence the disadvantage of the sectional method for permanent remembering.

While we may take it as generally true that the entire method is, within limits not yet determined, the best method of learning by heart, there is one important qualification which must be emphasized. The principle holds only for homogeneous or nearly homogeneous material. If the material to be learned presents special difficulties at different parts, these parts may resist learning long after the rest of the material has been mastered. Consequently the entire method, if slavishly followed in such a case, will mean a greater waste of time the longer the piece, since it will involve the needless repetition of what has been already learned. The better procedure is to read over once or twice to begin with, until we have discovered the specially difficult parts, then concentrate attention on them until they have been mastered, and finally master the whole piece by reverting to the entire method.

CHAPTER XII

IMAGINING AND THINKING

THIS chapter must be devoted largely to defining and distinguishing. This is necessary if we are to get a clear notion of the various intellectual processes that take place at, and mental elements that are characteristic of, the higher mental levels. As in our discussion of remembering we have already passed beyond mere perception, the task of defining and distinguishing must be undertaken now. The general mental processes at levels higher than the perceptual, exclusive of remembering, we call imagining and thinking. The technical terms are : *ideal representation*—which would include remembering—and *intellection*. In the same way as the product of the perceptual process is the percept, so the product of ideal representation is the image or train of imagery, and the product of intellection the concept, judgment, or, more generally, train of thought. Or, to put the matter more simply, in imagining and thinking the mind is active by way of images and ideas, as in perceiving it is active by way of percepts.

The nature of the percept has already been considered. An image is a revived perceptual experience in the absence of any immediate affection of our sense organs. It is not quite accurate to say it is a revived perceptual experience, for it is not a perceptual experience. But by means of the image we can apprehend an object which is not at the time affecting our sense organs. We can have before the mind's eye an object we saw yesterday ; we can apprehend ideally a situation we apprehended perceptually a month ago, a year ago, in early childhood.

The first question we are naturally prompted to ask is : in what respects does the image differ as an experience from the percept. As a general rule we do not confuse our images with our percepts in everyday life. We have usually no difficulty in distinguishing between, say, a real orange which we see before us, and an orange which we merely imagine. Hence there must be some difference between the two experiences. What the difference is, however, is a question somewhat more easily asked than answered. We can specify several distinguishing marks, which are generally found, but we cannot mention one that may not on occasion fail.

In the first place the image is usually less vivid than the percept, and usually also it is less full of detail, that is to say, more sketchy. But this is by no means invariably the case. A percept may be very faint and indistinct, so that we are not certain whether the experience is of a real object or not, as, for example, in the case of the hearing of a faint sound. On the other hand an image may be very vivid and distinct, so that we are almost deceived into taking it for reality.

In the second place, image and percept are differently related to our activity. We can control our imagery in a way we cannot control our percepts. We may control our percepts to some extent but only by controlling our position and movements. Our percepts depend on our position and movements, and inevitably change with them. Take, for example, our visual experience of a landscape. The particular aspect we see depends on the direction in which we look, and we can control that, but any change of the direction in which we look, any movements of the eyes, or head, or body, having that effect, change our perceptual experience in spite of our wills. It is not so with the image. We can revive our experience of that landscape, and any aspect of it, quite independently of our position and movements at the moment. We can have the image with our eyes shut, or stretched in an easy chair by the parlour fire. Further, owing to the control we can exercise over the image, we can ideally represent things as different from what they really are, even when we are perceiving the things. That is to say image and percept are relatively independent of one another. We cannot see an object red and blue at the same time, but we can image it as red, while perceiving it is blue.

In the third place the perceived object has usually a definite perceptual setting ; the imaged object, on the other hand, is detached. An object actually seen is seen in a definite context, and the context consists, not only of the surrounding objects as seen, but of the total sense experience at the time, the whole yielding us apprehension of a situation, into which the object we perceive fits. The image is detached from, and independent of, the sensory context, except in cases where images share in the perceptual process as a whole, and even in this case there is the same detachment, though it is not so apparent. For example, in a game of combat, like football, where success depends on our acting immediately on the perception of a movement on the part of an antagonist, we may anticipate, by means of an image of some movement we expect an opponent to make, an experience which is coming. The experience, when it comes, may be practically identical with, or differ considerably from, the image. No matter how well or ill our anticipation may fit into the actual series of events, the anticipatory image is always detached from the particular perceptual experience of the moment, and a series of anticipatory images is similarly detached from the series of percepts. Normally this distinction is clear enough. But there are cases where the image itself so dominates consciousness, that the sensory context sinks into insignificance, in which cases the criterion would fail.

In the fourth place, perceptual experience comes to us with a kind of ' challenge.' We are, as it were, challenged to make the necessary adjustments, in view of this or that particular external condition. This ' challenge ' must be regarded as one of the essential elements in that ' feeling of reality ' which is at the basis of belief, and which marks off for us the real from the merely imaginary. In this connexion, however, it must be remembered that, when we wish or expect to act in any particular way, there is a tendency for us to experience this 'challenge,' and therefore to have the 'feeling of reality,' where there is no corresponding objective reality.

Such are the main characteristics which mark off in our experience the image from the percept. They may all fail, but that is a point for consideration later. It is now necessary for us to attempt to distinguish an image from an idea. This distinction is somewhat more subtle. The word 'idea' may be used in either of two senses, a wider sense and a narrower sense. In the wider sense it is equivalent to any thought we may have of any object. The word is not really required in this sense, and is simply confusing. In the narrow sense it is used to signify the thought of an object in the absence of the object itself, and it is in this sense that it must be distinguished from 'image.'

In the ordinary course of our remembering and thinking, when we are reviving past experience, our past experience comes to us in the shape of images. But there is always a web and woof of relations and images together. We may not be concerned with the images for themselves at all, but with a certain 'meaning' which they symbolize for us, or with certain aspects of them, which have significance in the particular connexion. In such a case our experience is a train of ideas, rather than images. The idea implies the image, but is not itself the image but the 'meaning' for which the image stands. Here is an example from Stout. In a certain train of thought the idea of death occurs. The image before the mind, which symbolizes death, may be that of a dead bird. We are not, however, interested in the image for itself, but in its 'meaning,' death, which is what is relevant to the train of thought. An artist painting a picture of death, symbolized by a dead bird, would attend mainly to the details of the image. His interest and attention would, therefore, pass from the idea to the image, whereas ours do not dwell on the image at all but on the idea.

The distinction may seem a fine one, but it is nevertheless worth drawing. Another example of a different type will perhaps emphasize the reality of the difference. For the most part the thinking of the educated adult, and a good deal of his remembering, is carried on by means of verbal or word images. When he thinks of a horse, he mentally speaks or hears the word ' horse,' or sees it as printed ; when he thinks of immortality he similarly speaks, hears, or sees the word ' immortality.' In that case the image in itself has no interest of its own at all, and the meaning is practically everything, so that ' idea ' is obviously the right term to use. Whether we can ever have ideas without any imagery of any kind is a disputed point in psychology, but it is certain that the image may be exceedingly vague, indistinct, and unimportant, while the idea is definite, clear, and essential.

Our next task is to distinguish remembering, which we have already considered, from imagining, which we have still to discuss. The most fundamental distinction between the two processes is with respect to their respective relation to what is apprehended as real and independent of us. Remembering is determined by the fact or event, to which the course of ideal representation must adjust itself. The train of images or ideas reproduces and represents a series of experiences we have had, and therefore real occurrences. It is the consciousness of this that makes us say we remember. Without such consciousness there is no remembering as far as we are concerned. This is a kind of constraint placed upon our ideal representation. Our ideal representation must follow the lines laid down by the series of events to which it refers. Moreover, the fact or event is past, and is therefore completely determinate, irrevocable, unalterable. Other forms of ideal representation are in varying degrees free from this restraint, if we may so express it. As contrasted with remembering, expectation represents one degree of freedom, since, while the ideal representation still refers to an independent real, it is a real that is not yet, that is therefore relatively indeterminate, and may eventuate this way or that way. In planning for the future a further degree of freedom is exemplified, because the making of plans involves the possibility of partial determination of the future by us.

The highest degree of freedom is exemplified in day-dreaming, or mere play of fancy, when there may be no conscious reference to the independent real as such at all.

A second characteristic difference is that remembering is predominantly reproductive of an experience we have had, imagining predominantly constructive of a new experience, while other forms of ideal representation combine the two in varying proportions.   Construction in ideal representation must be rightly understood.   It does not mean the construction out of nothing of new elements of experience, but the free employment and combination of elements derived from perceptual experience in new ways.   That is, no one can construct in imagination a colour who has never seen a colour, or a musical note who has never heard a sound ; but the artist can combine colours he has seen into colour schemes he has never seen, and the musician can combine notes he has heard into tunes he has never heard.

There are three main types of constructive process : (a) processes of separation or subtraction, when parts of a perceived situation are represented without their perceptual setting or surroundings, as in imagining a house, or a tree, or a ship, separate from the other elements in the situation in which we perceived them ; (b) processes of combination and addition, where new elements are represented as added to or combined with perceptual situations as experienced, as in imagining a wing added to the house, leaves to the tree, funnels to the ship ; (c) processes of substitution, where one part is substituted for another, or one element for another, from the same or a different perceptual experience, as in imagining a river instead of a road running past the house, a seat instead of a bush under the tree, a lifeboat instead of a tug by the side of the ship.

In imagining, therefore, we revive past experiences, as in remembering, but, so far as we are merely imagining, the feeling of fact or reality is absent, and there is no identification with our past.   The various elements revived may be combined into wholes in accordance with our purpose at the time, and these wholes, so far from representing what we feel to be fact or reality, may be wholes never before experienced either by ourselves or any other person. Imagination is relatively, and to a varying extent in different cases, free from the trammels of the world of fact.

Various forms or kinds of imagining can be distinguished. First of all constructive imagination shows two forms. It may be either imitative or creative, according as the imagining is carried out after a pattern laid down by somebody else, for example by describing an event or scene in conversation or in the pages of a book, or according as the imagining is carried out after a pattern determined by ourselves. Further, both imitative and creative imagination may be either æsthetic or pragmatic. This is a very important distinction, too often neglected, which cuts very deep into our whole mental life. In pragmatic imagination the whole process is carried on with reference to a definite end, which gives the process its significance and value, and this end is determined by the conditions of the real world, so that the whole process is so far bound down to the conditions of real existence. In æsthetic imagination, on the other hand, the process is carried on largely for the satisfaction which it yields, and the end is largely— it may be wholly—a self-imposed one, so that the activity is free from the limitations imposed by the conditions of real existence to a far greater extent, it may be entirely. The first form is best illustrated by the imaginative process of the engineer, planning a bridge, the second by the imaginative process of the artist, poet, or novelist. The pragmatic imagination presents two distinct types, which may be called practical and theoretical, according as our aim is the doing or the undertaking of something. The æsthetic imagination may vary from the purely fantastic, through the artistic, to the idealistic, in which it abuts on the pragmatic.

While the æsthetic imagination is undoubtedly of great importance in human life, both because of the pleasure it involves, and because of its elevating influence, especially in the artistic and idealistic types, the pragmatic imagination, which we do not usually recognize as imagination at all, is, contrary to general opinion, of still greater importance for our everyday life. All our planning and purposing, all our efforts to realize scenes and conditions we have never directly experienced, all our attempts to enter into the thoughts and feelings of other people, involve this latter form of imaginative process.

In the view of the man in the street pragmatic imagination would probably be identified with thinking, rather than with imagining, but it is not thinking in any strict sense, in the sense, that is, of intellection. Thinking proper is characterized by the apprehending of relations. In thinking we discriminate the aspects of concrete experience, whether perceptual or imaginatively realized, we note resemblances and differences, compare, generalize, and reason. In all this the fundamental fact is that we actively pass in experience from object to object, at the same time holding the objects together and thinking their relations. This kind of activity is also generally involved in our ordinary remembering and imagining, but it is different from remembering and imagining; it deals with meanings, ideas, concepts, not percepts or images.

This thinking of relations gives us a new kind of freedom and a wider mental sweep. In our perceptual experience we are bound down to the present moment, and to those things affecting our sense organs at the present moment. Our ideal representation frees us from both these limitations. We can recall the past ; we can expect and forecast the future ; we can modify and recombine the perceptual elements in all kinds of new ways. But our ideal representation is still confined to particular concrete experiences. The thinking of relations frees us from this further limitation.

Let us try to make this point clear, because it is important. We have perceptual experience, say, of a yellow, round object (an orange) lying on the table. We can ideally represent the same object, or introduce all kinds of modifications. But in every case we are dealing with definite, particular, concrete experiences. When, however, we think of the object before us as having the qualities ' roundness ' and ' yellowness,' and as being in a certain position, expressed by the preposition ' on,' relatively to the table, note what is happening. We are discriminating aspects of the concrete experience, 'roundness,' 'yellowness,' 'on-ness,' which may also be aspects of numberless other experiences. We are also apprehending the relations 'being a quality of,' and 'being in a position as regards,' which are quite general relations, and in no sense bound down to the present concrete, though thought in connexion with it. It is but a step now to go on to compare objects with respect to yellowness, roundness, etc., and to think of yellowness, roundness, and so on, apart from any particular object. The thinking of relations thus enables us to have that kind of experience called a concept, and to go on to deal with concepts, independently of the particular and the concrete, to go on, it may be, to the discovery of laws and principles which are universal.

This development of mind seems to be reached by the human being alone to any significant extent. It is accompanied by another development, also characteristic of human beings alone—the development of language. The two developments are mutually dependent. No considerable development of conceptual process is possible without some kind of language, and there is no need for language apart from conceptual process. Animals do not speak, some one has said, not because they cannot, but because they have nothing to say. It is by means of language that we normally carry on the process of thinking for ourselves, and it is by means of language that we direct the remembering, imagining, and thinking of other people along the lines we desire. Language enables us to separate out the aspects of any given experience, to express the relation between these aspects, and to construct the total experience for another person, so as to enable him to understand it, and even to ideally represent it.

Let us illustrate once more. We say to a child : " There is an apple on a plate in the dining-room for you." Each word used expresses an aspect or a relation, distinguished by us in a given concrete experience, and the arrangement of the words in the sentence brings each aspect and relation into the mind of the child, in such a way as to enable the whole to be reconstructed, so that the child can ideally represent the situation and act accordingly.   Consider in contrast to this a hypothetical case of animal behaviour.   A mouse finds a store of cheese in a cupboard, and summons her family and friends to partake of the feast, let us say by various scamperings and squeakings.   Are we to regard these scamperings and squeakings as language ?   Only if, instead of being merely general expressions of excitement and delight, tending to make the other mice rush excitedly to the spot, they are each definite signs expressing definite aspects and relations in the presented situation, and enabling the other mice to ideally reconstruct the situation in some measure, before they have perceived it.   This, from our whole knowledge of the behaviour of mice, we have no reason to suppose they are.

Although we have described the processes separately, it must be kept in mind that in the complexity of our everyday experience remembering, imagining, and thinking all go on together.   In particular our remembering is very seldom without some thinking, though our imagining may perhaps be more often without any significant thinking, and our thinking is never without some remembering and imagining. In all cases there is a flow or train of images or ideas, or both, and while the succession in this train may be determined by association, it is guided and controlled by selective attention and active thought, in the service of our purpose or aim at the moment.

CHAPTER XIII

ILLUSIONS, HALLUCINATIONS AND DREAMS

AN illusion may be defined as " a subjective perversion of the objective content of sense perception." We have already seen that the subjective or inner factor is always highly important in perceiving, and very often becomes predominant. It can give rise to no surprise, therefore, that we sometimes perceive wrongly, that we take things for other than they are. Such erroneous perceiving is called ' illusion.'

Some illusions are more or less constant and practically universal. Others vary with our emotions and our moods, our interest and our attention. Among the familiar constant illusions are the so-called geometrical optical illusions. As a rule we cannot help seeing a vertical line as longer than a really equal horizontal line, and thus a mathematically perfect square always seems too high for its breadth. Under certain conditions really straight lines will appear curved, really parallel lines inclined to one another, and in spite of the fact that we know the true state of matters, we cannot help seeing the false. In the same way we cannot help feeling a small object heavier than a similar but larger object of equal weight, even when we know the weights to be equal. Illusion must, however, be clearly distinguished from delusion. Delusion is a matter of judgment or belief, not merely of perception. We may have illusion without delusion, and delusion without illusion, though on occasion illusion may give rise to delusion and delusion to illusion. Many illusions are so much a matter of everyday experience, and so well known, that we are not deceived by them, and think right though we perceive wrong. In these cases the deception of our senses is of relatively small importance. There are other cases, however, where such deception may exercise a profound influence on our lives, and not always a beneficent influence. Illusions determined by our desires and emotions and initiating actual delusions—erroneous judgment added to false perception—are of such a character. Examples of such illusions on a vast scale are afforded by the operation of social suggestibility in the epidemics of witch hunting and demonophobia of the Middle Ages, and various religious and spiritistic movements of our own time.

After our discussion of the influence of the inner or subjective factor in perceiving, there is little to add that is of fundamental psychological importance. Apart from the illusions to which all human beings are subject, the geometrical optical illusions, the size-weight illusion, and the like, the most important factors leading to particular illusions in individual cases are what we may designate generally as habit—a customary way of looking at things, or reacting to things—and feelings or desires, operating at the time when we have the illusion. Whatever the cause of the illusion may be there is always some sense basis. A real object is present, though it is apprehended as other than it is. Otherwise we are not dealing with an illusion, but with a hallucination.

A hallucination is a rarer, more striking, and psychologically equally important kind of false perception. In hallucinations we have perceptual experiences, which have either no sense basis at all, or an utterly inadequate sense basis. The criteria which differentiate image from percept apparently fail us, and we take for a real object what is a mere figment of the mind. There is really no sharp line of demarcation between illusion and hallucination, but they merge into one another, the more extreme forms of illusion being with equal appropriateness regarded as hallucinations. Nevertheless, it is convenient to assume that they can be sharply distinguished in the way we have suggested.

Illusions are ordinary phenomena of everyday life. It is

interesting to inquire whether there is any experience of our normal waking life which approximates in character to the hallucination which is admittedly somewhat abnormal, any case where a purely subjective factor determines perceptual experience without any sense basis. Dreams would apparently serve our purpose as an analogy, but these we are reserving for consideration later. The filling in of the blind spot in vision seems a sufficiently near analogue. We receive no visual sensation whatever from the part of the retina where the optic nerve enters the eye. Consequently, with the eyes motionless, there should be corresponding gaps in our field of vision. But we are not conscious of any such gaps. When we investigate the matter under experimental conditions, in order to determine what actually takes place, we find that we fill out the blind spot subjectively, by continuing, as it were, the sensation received from the surrounding area over the blind spot. This is plainly of the nature of a hallucination, in so far as it is perceptual experience without any sense basis. The opposite state of matters also is not infrequent— that is inability to perceive an object when it is affecting the sense organs. As already pointed out, in reading we read a line by rapid shifting of the fixation point along the line, the actual reading being done while the eye is at rest. During movement of the eyes we ought to see the letters blurred, as we see the upright posts of a fence when passing rapidly in a railway carriage. We are entirely unconscious of any such experience. The blurring effect is subjectively suppressed, or dissociated. This is a very good analogue to the phenomenon known as the 'negative hallucination.'

In the hypnotic condition both positive and negative hallucinations are ordinary phenomena, though the positive have mostly some kind of sense basis, and there are all gradations from the simple illusion to the unmistakable hallucination. Some of the negative hallucinations are very striking. The hypnotist says to the subject, speaking of one of the persons present, " Mr. A. has left the room. Go and take the chair he has vacated." The subject immediately ceases to perceive Mr. A., and attempts to sit down on the

9

chair on which he is sitting. Moreover, as long as the suggestion is not removed, the subject is deaf as well as blind to
Mr. A. Anything he says is as if it had not been spoken.

The explanation of the negative hallucination in terms of
dissociation is simple enough, though the explanation of how
the dissociation takes place may in certain cases be far from
simple. The genesis of the positive hallucination presents
a more difficult problem. What requires explanation is how
a figment of the mind can take on sensational character.
Two explanatory theories have been put forward. According
to the first the hallucination is always more than a mere
figment of the mind, because there must be actual stimulation
of a sense organ. According to the second, processes in the
nervous centres are themselves sufficient to explain the sensational character without any actual stimulation of the sense
organ. Some adherents of the first theory have maintained
that obscure stimulation of a sense organ must be present
as the starting-point of the whole process, that is, that hallucinations are always in principle reducible to illusions. The
form the hallucination takes is due to subjective conditions,
but without the original sense stimulation there could be
no hallucination. Now there can be no doubt that a great
number of hallucinations can be accounted for in this way.
Hallucinations may be confined to one side. Voices are heard
only on one side ; a figure is seen only when one eye is open.
In many such cases it has been shown that there is some
irritation of the inner ear, or some abnormality of the refract-
ing media of the eye. But it is difficult to account for other
hallucinations in this way. Hallucinations may start with
one sense and come to involve others as well. Thus in
delusional insanity the patient may begin by hearing voices
and end by seeing the owners of these voices. It seems that,
in order to account for phenomena of this kind, we must
supplement the morbid irritation theory by maintaining
that sense stimulation may also be produced as a result of
central excitation, and that it is only when it is produced
that we have the hallucination. Thus we may have a vivid
image to begin with, but that may have the effect of stimulat-

ing the sense organ, when the vivid image will become a hallucination, though previously it has been nothing more than a vivid image.

The mechanism of hallucinations according to the opposing theory has been described by James with his usual plausibility. Arguing on a physiological basis, he maintains, first, that sensations and images are due to the activity of the same nervous centres ; secondly, that in the case of sensation there is a peculiar intensity of nervous discharge, which is absent in the case of images, because of the fact that energy is being continually drawn off along association paths ; and, thirdly, that with the blocking of these paths there may be an accumulation of energy, which ultimately leads to a discharge having sensational intensity even though the occasion of the discharge is only an image. Hallucination is produced in such a case because the process in the nervous centre is identical with that of a perceptual experience. The theory, it must be confessed, is highly speculative, but nevertheless is not without advantages. It would make positive as well as negative hallucinations dependent upon dissociation, and it would seem particularly applicable to those hallucinations we call dreams.

While there may be some difficulty as regards the genesis of hallucinations, the conditions favourable to their development are easily specified. Apart from the factors upon which the sensational character of the hallucination directly depends, the favouring conditions fall into two groups— emotional, and organic, we may call them. The most important condition of all is a favourable emotional state. This is shown most clearly in the hallucinations of the insane. The malady begins, let us suppose, with delusions of persecuton. Then the patient whenever he sees two people speaking together begins to imagine that they are speaking about him, abusing him or plotting against him. Then follow auditory hallucinations of voices abusing him, and ultimately there may also be visual hallucinations of the persons to whom the voices belong. The main determining condition throughout is the subjective delusion of persecution. Hallucinations with this kind of determining condition are always abnormal phenomena, but it is not necessary to go for illustrations to the records of insanity. Overwhelmingly strong emotions —fear, grief, and the like—are capable of producing this result with individuals otherwise sane, the emotions playing the same part as the delusions in the case of the insane.

The other group of conditions is exemplified by conditions like fatigue, the oncoming of sleep, the influence of drugs, and the like. Fatigue brings about a state in which hallucination is readily produced. A fairly frequent type of hallucination due to this condition takes the form of revived perceptual experience as a kind of after-sensation. Thus, after a dance, the music often keeps ringing in the ears with hallucinatory vividness, when we get home and try to get to sleep.

But, after all, hallucinations must be regarded as abnormal, and scarcely as matters of everyday experience. The main reason why we have discussed them in such detail is to lead up to those hallucinatory experiences which occur during sleep, and which we call dreams. These at least are not abnormal. The number of people who have experienced hallucinations in waking life may be small—the census of hallucinations taken by the Society for Psychical Research proves it to be larger than generally supposed; but the people who have experienced, and who nightly experience, hallucinations during sleep cannot be numbered even in millions.

We are in great part ignorant both of the physiology and of the psychology of sleep. According to the ordinary view, perfectly sound sleep is the antithesis of consciousness. If we take this to mean that in perfectly sound sleep there is nothing of the nature of psychical process, then such a view is very difficult to maintain, and what evidence we have points all the other way. If it is true, perfectly sound sleep must be an exceedingly rare condition. The best way to regard sleep from the psychological standpoint is in terms of dissociation, rather than in terms of unconsciousness, the extent of the dissociation varying with the soundness of the sleep.

Whether sleep necessarily involves dreaming is also matter of dispute. Such evidence as we have seems to point that way, though from the nature of the case it is difficult to get conclusive evidence either way. Certainly many people assert that they never dream, but such statements can hardly be accepted as conclusive. In the case of the deeper hypnotic states, the subject after waking to normal consciousness is without the slightest trace of recollection of what transpired in the hypnotic condition. Yet in that condition the most lively mental activity may have been manifested. Arguing on the analogy of these deeper hypnotic states, it would seem to be impossible to obtain evidence of dreaming in the soundest sleep. On waking any such dreams would almost necessarily be forgotten. As a matter of fact the dreams we remember and relate are usually the dreams we have had just before waking, and consequently dreams that occurred in light sleep. It is to be expected that the greater the dissociation the greater the forgetfulness. Moreover, if they are not related or recorded immediately, dreams as a general rule fade rapidly from memory.

If dreams are regarded simply as hallucinations occurring during sleep, the same account may be given of their genesis, and the same theories will apply. There is ample experimental evidence, apart from general observation, that dreams may have their genesis in sense impressions, the actual form of the dream being subjectively determined, and the sense impressions having the most varied, and sometimes most extraordinary, elaborations and interpretations. The evidence also points to central excitation as a possible origin of dreams. *Mutatis mutandis*, therefore, most of what has been already said in this connexion concerning hallucinations will hold equally of dreams.

The analysis and interpretation of dreams has become an exceedingly important part of modern psychology. Surely no more interesting example can be found of the way in which the content of popular superstition in one generation

may become the content of science in another.   The new
dream-book is the textbook of psychology.   This is not the
least significant of the results of the work of Freud.   Attempts
to analyse and interpret dreams in a scientific way were
made long before Freud, but it was left to Freud to suggest
and to employ a new method of analysis and interpretation,
and this new method has revolutionized the whole psychological theory of dreams.   Prior to Freud it was known
that sense impressions during sleep entered into dreams, and
it was generally held also that all the content of dreams was
determined by the individual's experience and largely by
recent experience, but the particular, and often grotesque,
elaboration of the sense impressions and other content was
regarded as the product of chance, arbitrary and lawless in
the highest degree, and as such was left entirely unexplained,
without any effort even to explain.   One of Freud's fundamental positions, as we have seen, is that there is nothing
arbitrary or accidental in the mental life.   This is indeed a
postulate of psychology as a science.   It follows that the
wildest and most grotesque dreams are subject to psychological laws, equally with the most logical intellectual
processes.   It remains, therefore, for psychology to seek the
underlying laws, which will enable us to see order and causal
sequence in the phantasmagoria of the dream world.   Freud
has attempted, and undoubtedly with a large measure of
success, to formulate some of the more important of these
laws.

   The first principle of Freud's explanation is that every
dream is a wish-fulfilment.   The meaning to be attached to
the word ' wish ' requires to be carefully noted.   Ordinarily
by ' wish ' we understand appetitive tendency in its most
general form, so long as there is an idea of an object present
to a self.   It is a more general word than ' desire,' because
known impossibility of attainment will inhibit desire, while
the wish may still remain.   By ' wish ' Freud means this
general appetitive tendency, but he means more than this.
The general appetitive tendency we call ' wish ' always
implies for us a certain fairly high degree of mental synthesis,

since it implies the existence of personal consciousness. It is ' we ' who wish, not the tendency itself. In the case of successful repression of an appetitive tendency we should not say that we still wish the satisfaction of the tendency. On the other hand, Freud would include under the term the tendency itself seeking its satisfaction in such a case. Hence in the Freudian theory ' wish ' is to be understood of individual tendencies and complexes, as well as of the self as a whole.

A man who has strong leanings towards a military career is unable to gratify his desire, and under stress of circumstances is compelled to find employment and a means of livelihood as a man-servant in an hotel. During the day he cleans boots ; but every night he commands a regiment. Here we have simple wish fulfilment in the ordinary sense. But an equally simple case will show us the more elementary sense. A person suffering from thirst during sleep dreams of quaffing glass after glass of deliciously cool water. We seem to have here again simple wish fulfilment, but we really have more. By dreaming of quenching his thirst the individual is enabled to sleep on, at least until the thirst refuses to be assuaged by the dream water, and thus the ' wish ' represented in the tendency to sleep itself is gratified. In fact it is a second principle of Freudian interpretation that one of the functions of dreaming is to protect sleep. We shall return to the point presently.

The third principle of explanation introduces us to what is both theoretically and practically the most significant part of Freud's theory. He distinguishes between the ' manifest content ' and the ' latent content ' of a dream. The manifest content is the dream as it actually unrolls itself, the dream as it is related by the individual, apart from any secondary elaboration in relating it. The latent content is what the dream signifies or symbolizes—in other words its interpretation. In the two illustrations we have given the wish fulfilment is clearly shown in the manifest content of the dream, but the case is rarely so simple as this, and indeed few dreams present so much coherence and general rationality in their

manifest content. Usually the manifest content, even
where it is fairly coherent and rational, does not disclose
anything that can be interpreted as wish fulfilment, anything
at least which the individual is willing to interpret as wish
fulfilment. More often it is so far from being coherent or
rational, so absurd or grotesque, indeed, that to look to it
for wish fulfilment seems equally absurd. In such cases the
wish fulfilment is revealed in the latent content of the dream.
It is the latent content that gives the real meaning of the
dream ; it is the latent content that is the real dream.

Here is a very simple example of a dream where the
manifest content does not show wish fulfilment, and the
latent content does. " A young man dreamt that he stood
before a coffin in which his grandfather lay dead, and as
he stood there his grandfather's body moved and he turned
his head to one side and appeared to be uneasy." The analysis was that the grandfather represented the young man's
ideal. His ideal was dead, but did not rest easy in death.
In other words he was dissatisfied with the life he was living
and longing for some real, worthy work to do. This interpretation the dreamer immediately recognized as the true
one.[1]

But, if there is a reason for everything in the mental life,
there must be a reason why the real dream should so cloak
and disguise itself. The reason is that the wishes which
attain fulfilment in the dream are repressed wishes, and they
can only be fulfilled if they succeed in expressing themselves
in disguised form. In waking life a censorship is established
by recognized principles and standards, which secures that
these repressed wishes will be kept excluded from personal
consciousness. The censorship is to some extent abrogated
in sleep, but not sufficiently to enable them to enter the dream
consciousness undisguised. Moreover, in some cases they are
of such a nature that their entrance into dream consciousness
would inevitably and immediately wake us, and the sleep-
protecting function of the dream, therefore, demands that
they should be disguised. The disguise takes the form of

[1] White : " Mechanisms of Character Formation," p. 137.

condensation, distortion, displacement of the emotional element from where it really belongs, and an extensive use of symbolism.

The question may be asked : Is all this simply speculation ? It is not. In the Freudian theory as a whole there is some considerable amount of speculation, but so far as we have sketched it, it may be said to be based firmly on the facts revealed by dream analysis. The analysis is obtained by the methods of psychoanalysis already referred to. It may be a simple matter. On the other hand it may present almost, or quite, insurmountable difficulties owing to the fact that the censorship, which has compelled the wishes to disguise themselves in the dream, is in full exercise of its functions in waking life, and prevents these wishes from coming into the waking consciousness, in spite of all psychoanalysis can do. The forgetting of dreams and parts of dreams is itself interpreted by Freud as due to the influence of the same censorship.

It ought at the same time to be noted that many psychologists refuse to admit that repression plays the prominent part assigned to it by Freud and his followers. Jung, for example, maintains that dreams may have a compensatory function analogous to the function of some defence mechanisms already described, and in line with Freud's wish-fulfilment principle. Thus the sensitive and imaginative individual finds in the dream world a compensation for the commonplace drudgery and drab surroundings of his everyday life. The collection of children's dreams recently published by Dr. Kimmins[1] seem to give considerable support to this view. We need not, however, regard compensation and camouflage as alternative, but rather as complementary explanations.

There is one last point. If the Freudian theory is true our dreams must reveal the most intimate things in our nature and life. For this reason an individual would be wise to hesitate before relating a dream, especially if there is a psychoanalyst present. This is at the same time why dream analysis has come to be so important. From the individual's

[1] Kimmins : "Children's Dreams."

own point of view, the dream may often be said to show the course he ought to take to make his own life complete and harmonious. From the point of view of all who have the power or the duty of influencing the lives of others the significance of the dream is no less evident. Apart from the practice of the psychiatrist, there would seem to be a use for dream analysis in the problems which often face the clergyman, teacher, or parent ; in the practice of the psychiatrist dream analysis has already proved itself of the utmost value. Those repressed complexes which are at the root of so many mental and nervous disorders are revealed most easily by the analysis of the subject's dreams, and when they are revealed the question of treatment can be faced in a rational way ; until they are revealed all treatment is working in the dark. Moreover, that dreams sometimes reveal in an uncanny way things about to happen need not be so surprising, when we remember that they express the inmost tendencies of our nature.

NOTE.—It is difficult to understand what precise significance to attach to Freud's ' censorship.' A person's sentiments, principles, and whole character will undoubtedly exert an influence even in dreams on the thoughts that arise. Whether this will account for dream distortion is another matter. It must be remembered that common or similar feeling or ' affect ' may bring together many strange bedfellows from the point of view of waking conscious life. That being so, it is also apparent that the process of psychoanalysis may in some instances reduce itself to the tracing back of this affect, which fact must entirely alter the psychological status and significance of the analysis.

CHAPTER XIV

SPIRITISTIC PHENOMENA

IT seems desirable in a concluding chapter to take notice of some of the mysterious phenomena to which the spiritist appeals, not because these phenomena are themselves phenomena of everyday life, but because the interest in them may justly be regarded as a phenomenon of everyday life at the present time. It may be said at once that for some of the phenomena, as reported by the spiritist, psychology is as yet unable to account. The greater part of these, however, are phenomena which scarcely come within the scope of psychology, rather than, say, physics. Of the phenomena which do come within the sphere of psychology a few have already been touched upon in preceding chapters, and the psychological explanation indicated. It remains in the present chapter to consider briefly those others, not previously discussed, for the explanation of which psychology is at present willing to make itself responsible. Of these the chief are clairvoyance, automatic writing, and mediumistic possession. In all these cases the phenomena may be genuine, though there is no doubt whatever that they are often faked, and in all these cases the psychol gist has something to say, which it is well that the intelligent man in the street should listen to.

These and similar phenomena are more or less familiar to psychologists as manifestations of process in the 'unconscious.' We have several times had occasion to refer to the 'unconscious.' It now becomes necessary to explain more fully what that term means, and what psychical processes it

covers.   To begin with let it be granted quite freely that the
term is an unfortunate one.   All the conserved mass of
material representing past experience may rightly be called
' unconscious,' while it is conserved merely as dispositions.
All dispositions are unconscious.   Experiences alone are
conscious.   But the ' unconscious,' as employed in modern
psychology, covers more than dispositions ; it covers also
processes which are more or less of the same type as conscious
processes, processes of direct experience and of elaboration.
And the use of the word in this sense seems to imply that
conscious processes go on which are at the same time unconscious, and this is very like a contradiction, in fact very like
pure nonsense.   The difficulty is in part due to the fact that
we tend to confuse in thought consciousness with self-
consciousness.   There can be no doubt whatever that there
are conscious processes of which we are not *personally*
conscious or aware.   At least there are processes which are
of precisely the same kind as those which we should take
as evidence of consciousness in the case of other people and
in the case of the lower animals, which yet do not enter into
personal consciousness at all.   There are processes of such
a kind that, if we are not entitled to call them conscious,
then we can have no evidence of conscious process except
in our own immediate consciousness ; we can have, that is,
no evidence of consciousness whatever, as far as other people
are concerned.

We are sitting in a room reading, clearly conscious of the
book and the train of thought or story we are following,
vaguely aware of the light and the fire, not at all aware of
the ticking of the clock on the mantelpiece.   The ticking
stops, and we are immediately conscious that it has stopped.
Now obviously though we were not aware of the ticking, it
must have been exercising some kind of influence on the total
experience.   We must have been ' conscious ' of it below the
threshold of personal consciousness.   We meet an acquaintance and he tells us something.   What he tells us is in our
clear personal consciousness, but our whole awareness of
the situation may be influenced by something in his way of

telling it, his look, gesture, agitation or whatever it was, of which he was not conscious, and we were not conscious, but which nevertheless exercised such an influence on our total consciousness, that we found ourselves, we knew not how, ' instinctively ' distrusting the man and disbelieving his story.

Similar processes underlie numerous habitual and numerous absentminded acts in everyday life. It might be objected that habitual acts are more or less mechanical, and so far afford no evidence of accompanying conscious process. To some extent this is true. But there are numerous cases where slight deviations in the normal situation are adequately met and reacted to without the habitual series being disturbed, and without any intervention of personal consciousness ; and there are other cases where personal consciousness and personal control of action comes on the scene immediately on the failure of an act in the habitual series, in such a way as to prove conclusively that the habitual series was accompanied by conscious process of some kind throughout.

We have also already pointed out in a previous chapter[1] that an emotional disturbance may be represented in consciousness merely by a vague feeling with the organic disturbance. For example, in personal consciousness there may be indefinite anxiety or fear, which is the ' affect ' belonging to an idea or idea complex outside consciousness altogether. Yet that the idea or idea complex exists 'somewhere ' is proved by the fact that it can be brought into personal consciousness by the employment of appropriate psychoanalytic methods, and the results which follow when this is done.

But the clearest evidence of conscious process outside personal consciousness is that obtained from the study of more or less abnormal conditions, and it is here that the phenomena of the ' unconscious ' become closely similar to, if not identical with, so-called spiritistic manifestations. Such phenomena as those of post-hypnotic suggestion, where it is suggested to the subject during hypnosis, that some time after he has come out of the hypnotic condition, on a certain signal being

[1] See Chapter IV.

given, he will perform a certain action, and the whole process goes on to the performance of the suggested act without any personal awareness on the part of the subject, would afford a very good illustration of sub-personal conscious processes. From our present point of view it will be better, however, to take other illustrations bearing more closely still upon spiritistic manifestations, and more particularly the phenomena of crystal vision, automatic writing, and multiple personality.

First as to crystal vision. Crystal gazing is no product of modern times. It has been practised for centuries. The power of seeing pictures in crystals is by no means rare. In fact practically all good visualizers have the power, if they care to cultivate it. Hence, as regards the phenomena broadly, there is no real mystery about crystal vision, any more than there is about illusions, dreams, or hallucinations. Where the mystery comes in, if at all, is in the character of the pictures seen, and even that mystery is lessened, though it may not be entirely removed, by certain known facts regarding the 'unconscious' and the processes that may go on in the 'unconscious.'

The crystal gazer, looking into the crystal, sees pictures forming themselves there. The pictures may be recognized as representing familiar and remembered scenes and events. On the other hand they may not be recognized. As far as the personal consciousness is concerned they may present themselves as absolutely new experiences. In spite of the failure of the personal consciousness to acknowledge them, the evidence amply justifies the psychologist in holding that in every case, whether the individual personally recognizes the fact or not, they could be traced back to conserved experiences, if we knew everything, with the sole exception that there may possibly be pictures, the origin of which is to be traced to telepathy—as to that the psychologist in the meantime keeps an open mind. The essential point is that the psychologist has sufficient evidence to justify him in holding that psychological processes, and these alone, are involved in the phenomena.

One or two examples[1] will show the nature of the evidence. One of Dr. Morton Prince's patients, while on one occasion in the hypnotic state, smoked a cigarette with evident enjoyment. Later, in the normal state, she saw herself in a crystal, sitting on a sofa smoking the cigarette, and indignantly repudiated the lying vision. Here the original experience had never been in personal consciousness at all. It was nevertheless conserved, and reproduced as a visual image, though the eyes of the subject had been closed during hypnosis. Another crystal vision recorded by Morton Prince represented the subject walking in her sleep, writing letters, ascending the stairs again to her bedroom, and *unconsciously* dropping one of the letters on the stairs—the letter was found next morning by a servant. A third example may be given in Morton Prince's own words. " B.C.A., actuated by curiosity, looked into a crystal and saw there some printed words, which had no meaning for her whatever, and awakened no memory of any previous experience. It was afterwards found that these words represented a cablegram message, which she had unconsciously overheard while it was being transmitted over the telephone to the telegraph office by my secretary in the next room. She had no recollection of having heard the words, as she was absorbed in reading a book at the time. The correctness of the visual reproduction is shown * * * by comparison with the original cablegram."

Take now automatic writing. The phenomena of automatic writing were at one time fairly familiar through 'planchette,' which was in much vogue as a parlour game, and which was simply a particular device by means of which automatic writing could be secured. Automatic writing is writing produced without the subject being conscious of directing it, and sometimes without the subject being conscious that he is writing, although all the time he is fully awake. Usually the subject does not know what he has written until he reads it. Only some people can acquire the

---

[1] For most of the examples given in this chapter the author is indebted to Dr. Morton Prince's valuable book, "The Unconscious."

art, but it can be cultivated, and with hysterics and hypnotized subjects the phenomena are of frequent occurrence.

As in the case of crystal vision, there is a mass of evidence to show that what is written is derived from the past experience of the writer, though it may be experience which has never entered the personal consciousness at all.   Numerous illustrations could be given, for the literature of automatic writing is fairly extensive, but perhaps two will suffice. The first is quoted from Dr. Morton Prince once more and relates to the same subject as the last example of crystal vision.   " B.C.A. had been vainly hunting for a bunch of keys, which she had not seen or thought of for four months, having been in Europe.   One day, soon after her return, while writing a letter to her son, she was interrupted by her hand automatically and spontaneously writing the desired information * * * * * 'you put those keys in the little box where X's watch is.'   In explanation B.C.A. sent me the following letter : ' The keys were found in the box mentioned.   I had hunted for them ever since coming home.' "   As our other illustration we may select one which has a very distinct bearing on the use of the phenomena as evidence in favour of spiritism.   Two elaborate records of automatic writings have been kept and published, by Mrs. Verrall and by Mrs. Holland.   In one of the automatic writings of the latter, purporting to be a spirit message from a deceased friend, there occurred the sentence : ' Tell her this comes from the friend who loved cradles and cradled things.'   The exact words are found in a letter received by Mrs. Holland twenty years before, in which was given an extract from this friend's will, part of which ran : ' because I love cradles and cradled things.' Both letter and extract had been entirely forgotten, but, in the light of the evidence given by hundreds of cases of automatic writing there is no reason to suppose that Mrs. Holland's ' unconscious ' could not have conserved and reproduced the words without any spirit aid.

Lastly we may instance the strange phenomena of multiple personality, and allied conditions, as presenting features very similar to those of mediumistic possession, where these are genuine and not faked. Many cases of alteration of personality, and alternating or multiple personality, have been studied within recent times, and more particularly by the French psychologists. The most detailed description of such a case is given in Morton Prince's ' Dissociation of a Personality,' which describes a very interesting case—that of Miss Beauchamp—which came under his own observation and treatment. In cases like Miss Beauchamp's several different personalities seem to be inhabiting the same body— Dr. Jekyll and Mr. Hyde in real life. At any one time only one personality is, as it were, on the surface, and in charge of the conduct of affairs, but it is frequently possible by means of automatic writing to communicate with the other personality or personalities, even when submerged.

The relation of the personalities to one another may be somewhat intricate. Thus in the case of Miss Beauchamp there were three well-marked personalities, designated by Morton Prince BI, BIII, and BIV. BIII knew the inmost thoughts of BI, and was thus in a sense a continuous personality throughout the phases of BI and BIII, but she had no knowledge of the thoughts of BIV, while BI knew directly only her own experience. The three personalities were very different from one another in disposition and character, BI a pensive, nervous, conscientious person, BIII lively, mischievous, and hoydenish in the extreme, but good-natured and kindly, BIV proud, aggressive, and selfish. They differed also in intellectual acquirements ; for example, BI had a very sound knowledge of French, BIII did not know a word of the language, and BIV had a mere smattering. They differed even in physical health. The manner in which they alternated with one another sometimes became highly bewildering. BI might set out to consult the doctor, might change several times on the way to BIII or BIV, might enter the doctor's surgery as BI, and then change into BIV, who would have no idea of why she had come or how she had got there. Moreover, BIII could be communicated with by means of automatic writing when BI (say) was ' in the flesh,' or BIII could by suggestion be made to displace BI.

10

Numerous cases of this kind are on record. In some we have mere trance states, similar to the hypnotic trance, coming on spontaneously, lasting for a longer or shorter period and then disappearing, to leave the original personality without any knowledge of the trance period, or of what had happened during it ; in others we have the complete effacement of the whole previous life, and the necessity of starting afresh from the beginning even the acquiring of speech ; in still others we have complex conditions analogous to those of Miss Beauchamp. Of course there are, to some extent, analogous phenomena in normal life. The home personality, the social personality, the business personality of any individual may be marked by very different and even opposing characteristics.

The general lines of the psychological explanation are quite clear in all cases, and, though many details may still be unexplained, there is no reason to suppose that their explanation demands the assumption of spiritistic powers and agencies. That the phenomena are dissociation phenomena pure and simple there is no reason to doubt. If we regard them in this way we must suppose that all the words and acts of the different phases are controlled from within, and not from without, except so far as suggestion, and possibly telepathy, may be operating, controlled, that is, by what the subject has been or has experienced, either personally or subpersonally, at some time in the past.

All the phenomena which we have considered are phenomena largely exploited by the spiritist, and urged in support of opinions and beliefs which require the clearest and most cogent evidence before they can be accepted by any intelligent man. We have tried to show that the phenomena, or allied phenomena, are phenomena which the psychologist studies. And the psychologist claims that, if he has not solved all the problems, he is at least in a fair way towards solution. These are therefore matters regarding which psychology has, as Jastrow has put it,[1] " an authoritative charge to make to a public jury." The mere fact that an

[1] Jastrow : " Fact and Fable in Psychology," Preface.

eminent physicist or chemist has pronounced in favour of a spiritistic solution can carry no more weight than would be given in physical theory to the fact that a prominent psychologist had adopted a spiritistic theory of magnetic induction.   He would be a bold man who would attempt to define the limits of the possible, but the limits of the probable are easily determined by any intelligent man who is willing to acquaint himself with the relevant evidence, and to consider that evidence without personal bias or prejudice.

APPENDIX

THE HUNDRED 'BEST' BOOKS IN PSYCHOLOGY
FOR THE GENERAL READER

THE list of books which follows makes no claim to be an authoritative and standard list of the best books in psychology. It is merely an individual selection of those works which appear to the author most likely to be helpful to and interest the ordinary man. In some cases the selection is confessedly more or less arbitrary, so that in several instances other titles might be substituted without the value of the list being materially altered either way. The 'hundred' is also arbitrary, but some limit had to be fixed.

A. CLASSICS AND STANDARD WORKS.

1. Bain, Alexander. "The Senses and the Intellect." London, Longmans.
2. Bain, Alexander. "The Emotions and the Will." London, Longmans.
3. Bergson, Henri. "Matter and Memory." London, Allen and Co.
4. Berkeley, George. "A New Theory of Vision." Everyman Library.
5. Binet and Simon. "The Development of Intelligence." Trans. E. S. Kite. "The Training School." Vineland.
6. Carpenter, W. B. "Principles of Mental Physiology." London, King and Co.
7. Darwin, Charles. "Expression of the Emotions." London, Murray.
8. Galton, Francis. "Enquiries into Human Faculty." Everyman Library.
9. Hall, G. Stanley. "Adolescence." New York, Appleton and Co.

10. Hume, David. " Treatise of Human Nature." Everyman Library.
11. Hutcheson, Francis. " Essay on the Nature and Conduct of the Passions and Affections."
12. James, William. " Principles of Psychology." London, Macmillan.
13. Lewes, George H. " Physiology of Common Life." Edinburgh, Blackwood.
14. Locke, John. " An Essay concerning Human Understanding."
15. McDougall, William. " Body and Mind." London, Methuen.
16. Mitchell, William. " Structure and Growth of the Mind." London, Macmillan.
17. Myers, C. S. " Textbook of Experimental Psychology." Cambridge Univ. Press.
18. Reid, Thomas. " An Enquiry into the Human Mind on the Principles of Common Sense."
19. Sanford, E. C. " A Course in Experimental Psychology." Boston, Heath and Co.
20. Stout, G. F. " A Manual of Psychology." London, Clive.
21. Tarde, G. " The Laws of Imitation." New York, 1903.
22. Tucker, Abraham. " The Light of Nature."
23. Watson, J. B. " Psychology from the Standpoint of a Behaviourist." Lippincott and Co.
24. Whipple, G. M. " Manual of Mental and Physical Tests." Baltimore, Warwick and York.
25. Wundt, W. " Elements of Folk Psychology." London, Allen and Unwin.

B. Miscellaneous.

26. Adler, A. " The Neurotic Constitution." New York, Kegan Paul.
27. Allen, Grant. " The Colour Sense." London, Kegan Paul.
28. Ames, E. S. " The Psychology of Religious Experience." Boston, Houghton Mifflin Co.
29. Baldwin, J. M. " Social and Ethical Interpretations." New York, Macmillan.
30. Baudouin, C. " Suggestion and Auto-suggestion." London, Allen and Unwin.
31. Bergson, H. " Laughter." London, Macmillan.
32. Binet. " Psychology of Reasoning." Open Court Publishing Co.

33. Binet. " On Double Consciousness." Open Court Publishing Co.
34. Le Bon, G. " The Crowd, A Study of the Popular Mind." London, Fisher Unwin.
35. Brill, A. A. " Psychanalysis." Philadelphia, Saunders.
36. Cannon, W. B. " Bodily Changes in Pain, Hunger, Fear, and Rage." New York, Appleton.
37. Colvin, S. S. " The Learning Process." New York, Macmillan.
38. Drever, J. " Instinct in Man." Cambridge University Press.
39. Ellwood, C. A. " Sociology in its Psychological Aspects." New York, Appleton.
40. Freud, S. " Psychopathology of Everyday Life." London, Fisher Unwin.
41. Freud, S. " The Interpretation of Dreams." London, Allen and Unwin.
42. Freud, S. " Wit and its Relation to the Unconscious." London, Fisher Unwin.
43. Goodrich-Freer (Miss X). " Essays in Psychical Research." London, Redway.
44. Groos, Karl. " The Play of Man." London, Heinemann.
45. Hart, Bernard. " Psychology of Insanity." Cambridge Univ. Press.
46. Hobhouse, L. T. " Mind in Evolution." London, Macmillan.
47. Hollingworth and Poffenberger. " Applied Psychology." New York, Appleton.
48. Irons, D. " Psychology of Ethics." Edinburgh, Blackwood.
49. James, William. " Talks to Teachers." London, Longmans.
50. James, William. " The Will to Believe." London, Longmans.
51. James, William. " Varieties of Religious Experience." London, Longmans.
52. Jastrow, Joseph. " The Subconscious." Boston, Houghton Mifflin Co.
53. Jastrow. " Fact and Fable in Psychology." Boston, Houghton Mifflin Co.
54. Jastrow, Joseph. " The Psychology of Conviction." Boston, Houghton Mifflin Co.
55. Jung, C. " Psychology of the Unconscious." London, Kegan Paul.
56. Lay, W. " The Child's Unconscious Mind." London, Kegan Paul.

57. Lubbock, Sir John. "Ants, Bees and Wasps." London, Kegan Paul.
58. McDougall, W. "Introduction to Social Psychology." London, Methuen.
59. McDougall, W. "The Group Mind." Cambridge Univ. Press.
60. Marshall, H. R. "Pain, Pleasure and Æsthetics." London, Macmillan.
61. Meumann, E. "Psychology of Learning." New York, Appleton.
62. Moll, A. "Hypnotism." London, Walter Scott.
63. Morgan, C. Lloyd. "Animal Behaviour." London, Arnold.
64. Münsterberg, H. "Psychology and Life." Westminster, Constable.
65. Münsterberg, H. "Psychology and Crime." Westminster, Constable.
66. Münsterberg. "Psychology and Industrial Efficiency." Westminster, Constable.
67. Münsterberg and Others. "Subconscious Phenomena." London, Rebman.
68. Myers, C. S. "Mind and Work." London Univ. Press.
69. Nicoll, Maurice. "Dream Psychology." Oxford University Press.
70. Parish, E. "Hallucinations and Illusions." London, Walter Scott.
71. Peckham, G. W. and E. G. "Wasps Social and Solitary." London, Constable.
72. Pfister, O. "The Psychoanalytic Method." London, Kegan Paul.
73. Pillsbury. "Attention." London, Allen and Unwin.
74. Prince, Morton. "The Dissociation of a Personality." London, Longmans.
75. Prince, Morton. "The Unconscious." New York, Macmillan.
76. Puffer, E. D. "Psychology of Beauty." Boston, Houghton Mifflin Co.
77. Ribot, Th. "Psychology of the Emotions." London, Walter Scott.
78. Ribot, Th. "Diseases of Memory." London, Kegan Paul.
79. Ribot, Th. "Diseases of Personality." Open Court Publishing Co.
80. Ribot, Th. "Diseases of the Will." Open Court Publishing Co.
81. Ribot, Th. "Creative Imagination."

82. Rivers, W. H. R. "Instinct and the Unconscious."
Cambridge Univ. Press.
83. Ross, E. A. "Social Psychology." New York, Macmillan.
84. Scripture, E. W. "The New Psychology." London, Walter Scott.
85. Scripture, E. W. "Thinking, Feeling, Doing." New York, Putnam's Sons.
86. Shand, A. F. "The Foundations of Character." London, Macmillan.
87. Sidis, Boris. "Psychology of Laughter." New York, Appleton.
88. Sidis, Boris. "The Psychology of Suggestion." New York, Appleton.
89. Stratton, G. M. "Experimental Psychology and Culture." New York, Macmillan.
90. Stratton, G. M. "Psychology of the Religious Life." London, Allen and Unwin.
91. Sully, James. "An Essay on Laughter." London, 1902.
92. Sully, James. "Illusions." London, Kegan Paul.
93. Tanner, Amy E. "Studies in Spiritism." New York, Appleton.
94. Tansley, A. G. "The New Psychology and its Relation to Life." London, Allen and Unwin.
95. Terman, L. M. "The Measurement of Intelligence." London, Harrap.
96. Trotter, W. "The Instincts of the Herd in Peace and War." London, Fisher Unwin.
97. Valentine, C. W. "Experimental Psychology of Beauty." London, Jack.
98. Wallas, Graham. "Human Nature in Politics." London, Constable.
99. Watt, H. J. "The Foundations of Music." Cambridge Univ. Press.
100. White, W. A. "Mechanisms of Character Formation." New York, Macmillan.

INDEX

161